WITH US TODAY

On the Real Presence of
Jesus Christ in the Eucharist

Dearest Father Albert,

Thank you for drawing me closer to His Most Eucharist Sacred Heart.

your servant in Jesus,

Mary

WITH US TODAY

On the Real Presence of
Jesus Christ in the Eucharist

John A. Hardon, S.J.

Sapientia Press
of Ave Maria University

Nihil Obstat:	Monsignor John P. Zenz
	Censor Deputatus
Imprimatur:	✠Adam Cardinal Maida
	Archbishop of Detroit
	February 2, 2001

The *Nihil Obstat* and *Imprimatur* are official declarations that a book or pamphlet is free of doctrinal or moral error. No implication is contained therein that those who granted the *Nihil Obstat* and *Imprimatur* agree with the contents, opinions or statements expressed.

Published by

Sapientia Press
of Ave Maria University
Naples, Florida
888-343-8607
www.sapientiapress.org

Cover Artwork and Design: James Langley, Institute for Classical Art

Original Oil on Canvas is in a private collection in Steubenville, Ohio

Cover Graphic Production: Marie Shively

Printed in the United States of America
Library of Congress Card Number 00-110482
ISBN 0-9706106-0-2

TABLE OF CONTENTS

ACKNOWLEDGEMENTS

The author owes special thanks to many people without whom *With Us Today: On the Real Presence of Jesus Christ in the Eucharist* could not have been written.

- To Dominic Aquila, Diane Eriksen, Gary Zmuda and Tom Quirk of Ave Maria University Communications for their encouragement, editorial cooperation and patience.
- To John and Dolores O'Connell of Inter Mirifica for their diligent support of having the words of this sinner published in order to help teach the Catholic faith.
- To the Handmaids of the Precious Blood to whom I initially presented the contents of this book as a retreat.
- To Denyse Holguin and Gene Magney for their expert editing of the manuscript.
- To the Rev. Burns Seeley, SSJC, for his work in proofreading the final draft of the manuscript.
- To the Rev. R. Joseph Simburger for his help in assembling the present volume.
- To Kathy Stoeck for her work in finding applicable quotes from the saints.
- To Chris Murray for her research in coordinating sources and their authors.
- To Mrs. Raoul Holguin and Mrs. Ronald Schoenstein in their expert typing of the manuscript.
- To Dorie Gruss for her tireless efforts to ensure the present volume would be published in a timely fashion.
- To Mrs. Carol Egan, who completed the preliminary work for preparing a home correspondence course based on this book.
- To many others who, by their encouragement, counsel and active assistance, made this book possible.
- The best way I can express my gratitude is with my prayers, asking our Lord to bless them with an abundance of His choicest graces.

INTRODUCTION

The Eucharist is the center of Christianity. To understand the Eucharist is to begin to understand why God became man in the Person of Jesus Christ.

This book is an effort to express the Catholic faith in the deepest mystery of Christianity. We believe that God became man in the Person of Jesus Christ, but that is only the beginning. To believe in Jesus Christ is to believe that God became a human being, with flesh and blood, was conceived of His Virgin Mother Mary, born in Bethlehem and then for thirty years lived a hidden life in Nazareth.

He remained in total obscurity during those thirty years in Nazareth, realizing that once He would identify Himself as the Living God who became man, His death was imminent.

Jesus exercised His public ministry for only three years in Palestine. Not once, but many times, His life was in danger. Three years was only as long as He could remain alive by declaring Himself to be the Son of God who became man. Once His public ministry was complete, He allowed Himself to be betrayed by one of His own disciples, tried as an imposter and then crucified on Calvary. Once He allowed this, He remained alive for only one day. He chose to die at the hands of His enemies who belonged to the chosen people.

The night before He died, Jesus instituted the Holy Eucharist in order to remain alive as the God–man until the end of human history on earth. We, as Catholics, know that Jesus is truly present in the Holy Eucharist—

His Body, Blood, soul and divinity. Anyone who believes otherwise is not a Catholic.

It is impossible to exaggerate the importance of Christ's short life on earth between His conception and His death on Calvary. In the two thousand years since He died on the Cross, He has been crucified time and again by those who refuse to believe that the Living God became man, died out of love for us and remains alive for us in His Real Presence. This has been the history of Christianity for twenty centuries. He has died mystically many times since His Crucifixion. True enough, He died physically only once. But His enemies have crucified Him countless times ever since—including so-called Catholics who no longer believe in the Real Presence of Jesus Christ in the Blessed Sacrament.

The Christ in whom we believe is the Living God who became man to teach us the most important lesson we have to learn in life. We are only as faithful followers of Jesus Christ as we are willing to die like Him, with Him and for Him at the hands of the world who refuses to believe that the infinite God died on the Cross. We must be willing to die out of love for Him as He, our God, chose to become man to die out of love for us.

1

THE HOLY EUCHARIST, THE PRESENCE SACRAMENT

If there is one thing our Lord makes clear in the Gospels, it is the grave need of having our minds enter *into* what we believe. Remember the parable of the sower? Some seed fell on a path, some fell on rocky ground, some fell among thorns and some fell on rich soil. We know that only the seeds that fell on rich soil were fruitful.

We are also told that the first seedlings which fell along the pathway bore no yield because the birds of the air came and picked up the seed. When the disciples pressed Jesus to explain the parable, He said, "The seed sown on the path is the one who hears the word of the Kingdom without understanding it, and the evil one comes and steals away what was sown in his heart" (Matthew 13:19). Because they failed to *understand* the Word of God, the evil one came like a bird of prey and stole the Word of God from their hearts.

This should be etched in bronze: We need to have the Word of God not only sown in our hearts, but also sown in our *minds.*

We are living in the most critical era of the Catholic Church's history. Millions of once-believing Catholics have given up their faith. One diocese alone recently dissolved forty parishes in one year! There must be a reason. And there is.

The Catholic faith cannot just be believed to be retained. It must be understood. There is no option. We so frequently, and correctly, insist on developing the virtues of patience, charity, chastity, humility and obedience. But the one virtue upon which all the other virtues depend is faith. It is so important to remember this: We believe with the intellect. Either our minds are thoroughly convinced and our conviction keeps growing with increased intelligibility, or the inevitable happens—not only will the other virtues be weakened or lost, but faith itself will disappear. That is why the strength of the Catholic Church in any period of her history depends on the depth with which professed Catholics understand their faith.

Over the years, I have struggled with too many people, including priests and religious, to keep them in the faith. I have not always succeeded. You do not keep the faith today by being just an ordinary bishop, an ordinary priest, an ordinary religious, an ordinary father or mother, or an ordinary Catholic man, woman or child. Only heroic faith can withstand the pressures on the Catholic Church in our day. Given the widespread breakdown of once-flourishing Catholic parishes and dioceses and religious institutions, there must be a reason for this crisis. There is.

Weakening of faith produces weakening of commitment in the priesthood, in religious life, in marriage, in the family, in the laity and in all of Catholic society. As we see faith deteriorating all around us, we need to ask ourselves the basic question which underlies this whole issue. Is there one basic mystery whose weakening has been at the root of this crisis of faith? Yes, there is. The single most fundamental mystery of Christianity that mainly needs to be strengthened and deepened if we are to even preserve the Catholic Church in our day is "The Mystery of Faith" itself. It is the mystery of the Real Presence of Jesus Christ on earth today in the fullness of His divinity and the fullness of His humanity in the Most Blessed Sacrament of the altar.

WHY A BOOK ON THE EUCHARIST?

The Holy Eucharist will be the central theme around which all the reflections in this book will revolve. Our specific focus will be on the

Real Presence of Christ in the Blessed Sacrament in order that we might more clearly understand what we believe about the meaning of this most fundamental Mystery of Faith.

In this opening meditation, as we may call it, I would like to address two topics to set the stage for the book. First, we will draw on an important Papal encyclical titled, what else, *Mysterium Fidei*, "Mystery of Faith." Then we will outline our plan of twenty-six lessons concentrating on Christ's greatest gift to us on earth—Himself present in the Blessed Sacrament.

MYSTERIUM FIDEI

To appreciate why there is such a great need in our day to dedicate an entire book on the Holy Eucharist, we will look at Pope Paul VI's document *Mysterium Fidei*, published on September 3, 1965. What is historically unusual about this encyclical is that it was published during the sessions of the Second Vatican Council. This never happens. Popes *never* publish encyclicals during sessions of a general council. But Paul VI felt bound to express his concerns about erroneous Eucharistic teachings before the council closed.

The Holy Father began by saying he hoped the Second Vatican Council would inaugurate a new era of Eucharistic piety among the faithful. He earnestly hoped that rich fruits of Eucharistic devotion would grow out of the reformed Liturgy. He foresaw that "the Holy Church, under this saving sign of piety, may make daily progress toward perfect unity and may invite all Christians to a unity of faith and of love, drawing them gently, thanks to the action of divine grace." (6)

In paragraph after paragraph, the Pope repeated how hopeful he was that the Catholic Church of the future would be strongly liturgical because she is strongly Eucharistic. Then he expressed his main reason for publishing the encyclical during the Vatican Council. He explained how there are in circulation erroneous theories about the Eucharist, such as "transignification" or "transfinalization," as opposed to the Church's teaching of transubstantiation, which is the complete change of the substance of bread and wine into Christ's Body and Blood by a validly ordained priest during the consecration at Mass, so that only the appearances of bread and wine remain. Instead, the Pope said, writers "Propose and act upon the opinion according to which, in the Consecrated Hosts which remain after the celebration of the Sacrifice of the Mass, Christ Our Lord is no longer present. Everyone can see that the spread of these and similar opinions does great harm to the faith and devotion to the Divine Eucharist. And therefore, so that the hope aroused by the council, that a flourishing of eucharistic piety which is now pervading the whole Church, be not frustrated by this spread of false opinions, we have with apostolic authority decided to address you, venerable brothers, and to express our mind on this subject" (12). With his customary charity, the Pope does not impute bad intentions to the sowers of these false ideas. He presumes they are still sincere, but misled. However, he went on to say, "We cannot approve the opinions which they express, and we have the duty to warn you about the grave danger which these opinions involve for correct faith" (13).

That was 1965. Every single false opinion about the Holy Eucharist that Pope Paul VI mentioned—every one—has been amplified and circulated among the faithful since the publication of *Mysterium Fidei*. Every single anxiety he expressed in *Mysterium Fidei* has been traumatically verified.

I believe the center of the Church's crisis in the Western world in our day is the doubt and denial in an ever-widening circle of once-professed Catholics about their faith in the Real Presence. As a result, we see the massive desacralization of the Mass, the hidden tabernacles, the iconoclasm perpetrated on Catholic churches, the reduction of hundreds of churches to mere social meeting halls and the casual handling of the Sacred Species. These have all been censured by one Pope after another, but the devastation goes on.

BOOK OUTLINE

With this background, we are ready to briefly describe the approach we shall take in this book on the Eucharist. During the reflections, we will address three essential questions about this oceanic subject of the Real Presence:

1. What do we believe when we believe in the Real Presence?
2. Why did Christ institute the Holy Eucharist as His bodily presence on earth?
3. How are we to put this mystery of faith into practice?

Whether we are members of a domestic family of parents and children, or members of the clergy or members of consecrated life, the future of all family life depends on a deep and clear faith in the Real Presence. This book will help us better understand what we believe about the Holy Eucharist and why Christ gave us the Real Presence. Then we can more fully put this belief into practice. I have no doubt that if we take these reflections to heart and implement them in our individual lives, we shall make a major contribution to the sanctification of the Church, to our own sanctification and to the extension of Christ's Kingdom in the modern world.

But take note of what we are saying. Our concentration on the Real Presence is not a casual decision. There are many mysteries of the faith, but we have not just happened to choose this one. We focus on the Real Presence because the future of the Catholic Church in one Western country after another is on trial. More than thirty years in working for the Holy See has taught me many things. One thing I have learned is that the deepest and most devastating crisis in all the two thousand years of the Church's history is what we are undergoing now. The root of this crisis from one perspective is the priesthood and, from another perspective, is the Real Presence, for which the priesthood was mainly instituted by Christ.

Christ came to save the world from hell and for heaven, from sin and for grace. He died on the cross to redeem the world and win for us the graces of salvation. He continues today to confer and communicate those graces which He won for us on Calvary. This is what makes us Catholics: We believe Christ instituted the Church so that through the Church the graces of salvation might be communicated to a sin-laden world. The main source of these salvific graces is Christ Himself in the Holy Eucharist, and the foundation of the Eucharist is the Real Presence.

We can feel the gravity of this crisis of faith in the Real Presence when we consider the implications for the Catholic priesthood. The primary reason Christ instituted the priesthood was to perpetuate His Sacrifice of Calvary in the Sacrifice of the Mass. But the whole meaning of the Mass depends on faith in the Real Presence. Thus, without the Real Presence, there is no Mass. Without the Mass, there is no priesthood. Consequently, the whole of Catholic Christianity, the Catholic faith and the Catholic Church depend absolutely on the fact of the Real Presence.

In one declarative sentence: Without faith in the Real Presence of Christ in the Eucharist, there is no Catholic Church.

By way of exception, each section of the book will close with a short prayer. This is not an expression of excessive piety. It is because I am convinced that our intelligent grasp of the faith we profess depends, not only on our studying God's revealed mysteries, but asking Him for the light to understand His revealed truth.

P R A Y E R

LORD JESUS, AS WE START OUR READING ON THE SACRAMENT OF THE EUCHARIST, WE ASK YOU TO KEEP OUR MINDS ALERT. OPEN THE EYES OF OUR INTELLECT THAT WE MAY SEE MORE CLEARLY THAN EVER BEFORE AND SEE MORE DEEPLY AND MORE MEANING-FULLY WHAT YOU GAVE US WHEN YOU INSTITUTED THE HOLY EUCHARIST. YOU FULFILLED YOUR PROMISE OF REMAINING WITH US UNTIL NOW, AND YOU PROMISED TO REMAIN WITH US UNTIL THE END OF THE WORLD. DEAR JESUS, MAKE US UNDER-STAND THE REAL PRESENCE HERE ON EARTH SO THAT, BELIEVING IN YOUR PRESENCE WITHOUT SEEING YOU, WE MAY ONE DAY POSSESS YOU IN THAT ETERNAL EUCHARIST, WHICH IS THE BEATIFIC VISION FOR WHICH WE WERE MADE. AMEN.

2

THE TRUTH OF CHRIST'S REAL PRESENCE

Before we begin our analysis of the Holy Eucharist, we need to understand that Christianity is a historical religion. It is not mythology, like the religions of ancient Egypt, Babylonia, Greece or Rome. It is not the product of religious imagination, like Hinduism, Buddhism or the tribal religions of Asia, Africa or North and South America. Christianity is not a cult like Mormonism or Theosophy or Scientology or the New Age. Christianity has historical foundations, historical beginnings and a verifiable history over the centuries. It is no coincidence that by now the whole human race follows the calendar of Christianity, calculating its use of history from the birth of Jesus Christ, that is, from *Anno Domini*, the "Year of the Lord."

As the religion of history, Christianity has two levels of existence—its past and its present. On the level of the past, there were several main events which actually took place. Jesus Christ was really conceived by His Virgin Mother and was really born at Bethlehem. Mary held a real child in her arms. Jesus Christ really lived for thirty years at Nazareth. He really preached and worked real miracles. He walked with real feet on real water. He spoke with an audible voice when the dead Lazarus came out of the grave.

Jesus Christ really instituted the Eucharist and the priesthood at the Last Supper. He was really crucified, died, and, to make sure no one would ever doubt that He really died, He was buried. The moment He died, the Church was born. Jesus Christ really rose from the dead on

Easter Sunday, and He really ascended into heaven, body and soul, on Ascension Thursday. So far, that is the history of Christianity in the past.

Now on the level of the present: The Church which Christ founded really exists. It is not a speculative construct of the mind. You can tell who belongs and who is in charge. Moreover, the Jesus who really lived in Palestine, who really died, who really rose from the dead and ascended into heaven—that same Jesus is really on earth today in the Holy Eucharist.

Why is Jesus really present in the Holy Eucharist which He instituted at the Last Supper? Because the priesthood, which He instituted at the same time, exists on earth and is empowered to continue doing now what Jesus had done on that night before He died. It is impossible to exaggerate the reality, the factuality, the geographical exactness and the veracity of the Christian religion in its origins and in its present and continuing existence. There is a Real Presence because Christianity is real. Now we go on with our analysis.

WHEN DID CHRIST INSTITUTE THE HOLY EUCHARIST?

Before we talk about the actual institution of the Eucharist, it is important to know that Jesus often promised something and then fulfilled the promise. He said He would rise from the dead, and then He really died and rose from the dead. Similarly, as recorded in the sixth chapter of St. John's Gospel, Christ prepared His followers for the Eucharist by promising to give them His own Flesh and Blood as nourishment for the sustenance of the divine life conferred by Baptism. Then He fulfilled that promise at the Last Supper.

However, when He foretold the Eucharist, not everyone believed. But we should remember what St. Augustine says: We need unbelievers. They provide us with the opportunity of knowing more clearly what we believe. As recorded in St. John's Gospel, the unbelievers provided Christ with the opportunity of explaining the reality of the Real Presence He foretold He would give His followers. He explained how the supernatural life has to be nourished with His own Flesh and Blood and said He will give us His own Flesh to eat and His own Blood to drink. "Whoever eats My Flesh and drinks My Blood will have eternal life" (John 6:54).

The people who heard Christ speaking like this were astonished, even scandalized. They objected three times, and finally, some of the people, including many of his own disciples, left Him. "This is intolerable language! Who can believe it!" (John 6:62).

Yet so far from retracting or even qualifying what He had just said, Jesus repeated His promise of giving His own Flesh and Blood. He foresaw who in the future would not believe in the Eucharist. That is why in the same verse when Jesus spoke of those who do not believe, He said, "I know those who will betray Me" (John 6:65). Christ's worst enemies are those who had believed or had the faith offered to them and who by refusing to believe, became traitors. This includes Judas Iscariot, who later left the Last Supper. Not believing in the Real Presence, he went on to betray his Master.

Also in this Gospel scene, we notice that after a large number of His own disciples walked away, Jesus turned to the Apostles and asked them, "Do you also wish to go away?" They were all silent, except for Peter, who spoke up and said, "Lord, to whom shall we go? You are the Son of God. You have the words of eternal life" (John 6:68–69).

At the Last Supper, Christ fulfilled His promise. There are four narratives of His institution of the Holy Eucharist—in the evangelists Matthew, Mark and Luke, and surprisingly in St. Paul's first letter to the Corinthians.

Over the centuries, every major break with the Roman Catholic Church has been over the interpretation of Christ's words of institution of the Eucharist. Everything in Christianity depends on how we interpret what Jesus said at the Last Supper. By the year 1600, there were over two hundred interpretations among the Protestants. To this day, this is the main source of their division. It is also the principal cause for the modern crisis in the Catholic Church.

As we reflect on the institution of the Holy Eucharist, we must look closely at Christ's words at the Last Supper when He changed bread into His Body and changed wine into His living Blood.

Over the bread, Jesus says, "This is My Body which will be offered up for you." Note that the full text of the words of institution is not only "This is My Body," but "This is My Body which will be offered up for you."

Then over the chalice, Jesus says, "This is the chalice of My Blood of the New Testament which will be shed for many unto the remission of sins." Again, for us whose faith in Christ's Real Presence is the foundation of Christianity, we must make sure we know the full text of these words of institution. First He says, "This is the chalice of My Blood of the New Testament." Remember, there was blood shed in the Old Testament, but here, this is "*My* Blood" in the New Testament. Then He says, this is blood "which will be shed for you." Why is the blood shed for us? "Unto the remission of sins." Sin is removed by blood—the shedding of Christ's Blood on the Cross and the shedding of *our* blood physically if it is the divine will, but at least spiritually by the shedding of our wills in submission to the will of God.

Literal Interpretation. The Catholic Church has never wavered in her explanation of Christ's words of institution. These words of Jesus are historical. They were really spoken by Christ to the apostles. We know these words of institution were not spoken figuratively, but literally. We know this from the wording and language Christ used. There is nothing in the text of the words Jesus used which suggests a figurative or symbolic interpretation. Bread and wine are not flesh and blood either by their nature or by their use as symbols of speech in any language, either in Christ's time or in our own day. You have to read *into* the words of Jesus what the unbelieving mind thinks Jesus said.

In recent years, we have conveniently coined a separate word to distinguish exegesis from eisegesis. Exegesis means "drawing out" of the revealed text of Scripture the meaning intended by the Holy Spirit. The new word is "eisegesis." Eisegesis is reading *into* the Biblical text what is *not* there. Believe me, there are not a few biblical scholars who are widely read eisegetes today! But to use true exegesis, there is a presupposition. The precondition for taking Christ's words literally in this passage is faith in Christ's divinity and faith in the Church's infallibility. Only the infinite God could possibly say of what had been bread, "This is My Body." And of what had been wine, "This is My Blood." But you must believe that behind that human voice is the almighty power of the God who was and is Jesus Christ.

We also know Christ's words—"This is My Body . . . . This is My Blood"—must be interpreted literally because of the evident requirements in the situation when He spoke. In a matter of such paramount importance, the circumstances demanded that Jesus would not have recourse to meaningless, and worse still, deceptive figures of speech. Figures of speech enhance human discourse only when the figurative meaning is clear either from the nature of the case or from common usage, neither of which could be said of Christ's words at the Last Supper.

Because Jesus is a just God, He could not mislead the human race by using metaphorical language the night before He died in giving us the greatest legacy of His Incarnation. He did not allow any form of words that His followers might possibly misunderstand. Otherwise, Christ would have been an evil deity in promoting error among His followers on the Holy Eucharist, which is the most sublime mystery of Christianity.

Finally, we realize that only a literal interpretation is permissible when we read what St. Paul teaches about the unworthy reception of the Blessed Sacrament. Says the apostle, "Whoever shall eat this bread or drink from the chalice unworthily shall be guilty of the Body and Blood of the Lord, for he who eats and drinks unworthily does so to his own condemnation because he does not believe in the Body of the Lord" (1 Corinthians 11:29). There could be no question of a grievous offense against Christ Himself unless Paul assumed that the true Body and the true Blood of Christ are really present in the Eucharist.

Faith of the Early Christians. Belief in the reality of Christ's Body and Blood in the Eucharist goes back to the first Christians and is seen clearly in the writings of the earliest Church Fathers. There was no doubt in the mind of the early Church that what Christ instituted at the Last Supper was the Real Presence of Himself in the Eucharist. Significantly, all these testimonies of the Real Presence were made in defense of the Church's teaching against those who denied the literal explanation of Christ's words of institution. We shall limit ourselves to just three of the Church Fathers, all before the end of the second century.

Our first witness of the early Church is St. Ignatius of Antioch, who died in A.D. 107. This Church Father wrote against the heretics of his day, mainly the Docetists, who claimed that God did not really become man. In other words, the Docetists claimed that God took on the appearance of man but was not really human. Jesus did not assume a real human nature; He was only human in appearance. But faith in the Incarnation is the condition for our faith in the Real Presence, so we can see why the Docetists did not believe in the Eucharist.

Ignatius says, "They [the Docetists] keep away from the Eucharist because they do not believe that the Eucharist is the Flesh of our Redeemer, Jesus Christ, who suffered for our sins and whom the Father in His goodness raised from the dead." In writing against the Docetists, Ignatius provides us with a witness of the early Christian understanding of the reality of Christ's Presence in the Eucharist.

Our second witness, St. Justin the Martyr, wrote about A.D. 150. In this case, he wrote in defense of the Real Presence to refute those followers of Christ's contemporaries who walked away from our Lord when He foretold of the Real Presence. Speaking of the Mass, Justin says, "We receive [the Eucharist] not as ordinary bread or ordinary drink, but just as our Redeemer, Jesus Christ, became Incarnate by the Word of God and took on Flesh and Blood for the sake of our salvation, so as we have been taught the food which has been Eucharistized . . . is both the Flesh and Blood of that same Incarnate Jesus" (Apologia I, Chapt. LXVI of the Eucharist).

St. Justin draws a parallel between the Incarnation and the Eucharist. Just as truly as God became Man in Mary's womb at the Incarnation, so the same Incarnate Jesus becomes present on the altar at the moment of consecration in the Mass. In other words, the Eucharist *is* the Incarnation continued on earth until the end of time.

Our third witness is St. Irenaeus of Lyons. In *Adversus Haereses* (Against Heresies), written about A.D. 180, Irenaeus writes against the dissenters in his day to defend the Real Presence against those who had been Catholic but had given up the faith. "The bread over which thanksgiving (Eucharist) is pronounced is the Body of the Lord and the chalice of His Blood . . . . By His own Blood, He permeates our blood . . . and His own Body . . . strengthens our bodies" (4.18, 54; 5.2,2).

Then Irenaeus tells the Gnostics of his day (the "speculative" theologians) why they deny the Real Presence: "How can they feel assured that . . . the Eucharistized bread is the Body of the Lord, and the chalice contains His Blood if they do not declare Him to be the Son of the Creator of the world?" (4.18,4).

Truer words were never spoken. Both in the early Church and now, the ones who believe in the Real Presence of Christ in the Eucharist are those who believe Christ is the Incarnate Son of God in human form.

We can conclude with this simple statement: Only those who really believe that God became man can even begin to believe in His Real Presence now on earth in the Blessed Sacrament of the altar. Faith in the Incarnation is the foundation for our faith in the Real Presence. As a result, growth in our faith in the Incarnation is the condition for growth in our faith in the Real Presence.

P R A Y E R

LORD JESUS CHRIST, WE BELIEVE YOU ARE OUR GOD WHO BECAME MAN FOR OUR SAL-VATION. BECAUSE WE BELIEVE YOU ARE GOD INCARNATE, WE BELIEVE WHAT YOU SAID AT THE LAST SUPPER: "THIS IS MY BODY . . . . THIS IS MY BLOOD." WITH ST. PETER WE SAY, "TO WHOM ELSE SHALL WE GO? WHOM ELSE CAN WE BELIEVE IF WE DO NOT BELIEVE IN YOU, OUR GOD WHO BECAME MAN? YOU HAVE THE WORDS OF ETERNAL LIFE" (JOHN 6:69–70). AMEN.

3

History of Eucharistic Doctrine

Throughout the centuries, the Church's Eucharistic doctrine has been consistently occasioned by errors. In each case, one error was more subtle than the preceding. But there is a mysterious sense in which we can thank God's providence for drawing so much good and so much depth of truth from the errors propagated by those who deny a mystery of the faith. In God's providence, each error provided an opportunity for the Church's teaching to become even more clear and more specific.

In other words, heresy has contributed immensely to the sanctification of the Church. The more clearly the human mind understands what the mind believes, the more generously the human will can use what the mind knows is truth. For our purpose we hope to more clearly understand the truths of Christ's Real Presence in the Eucharist, so that we may give ourselves more generously to Him Who is present in the Blessed Sacrament.

We will look at the Church's teachings on the Eucharist in three eras: up to the sixteenth century, in the sixteenth century and from the sixteenth century up to modern times.

EUCHARISTIC DOCTRINE UP TO THE SIXTEENTH CENTURY

Our opening analysis covers the first fifteen hundred years of the Church's history. During this millennium and a half, there were three major Eucharistic heresies of which the Church not only took account, but also carefully refuted and explained her refutation. In the process, her teaching became more clear, more meaningful and more precise. All of these erroneous teachings came from once professedly Catholic sources.

The names of the originators or propagators of erroneous Eucharistic doctrine are standard in theology, although not so well known to the average Catholic believer. They are Berengarius, Durandus and Wycliffe. Their theories were condemned by the Church, and in each case, we see evidence of what we call "development of Eucharistic doctrine," which means a growth in the Church's penetration into the meaning of what Christ revealed when He instituted the Blessed Sacrament.

BERENGARIUS

There is no need to go into a detailed analysis of Berengarius's teaching on the Eucharist. It is enough to say that for the first thousand years of Christianity, there was no serious challenge to the accepted doctrine of the Real Presence of Christ in the Eucharist. What immediately provoked a controversy was the ninth-century publication of a work titled *On the Body and Blood of the Lord*. The author, Paschasius by name, was uncomfortable with the loose language some Christians were using to explain the Holy Eucharist. So he said, "after consecration [the bread and wine] are nothing else than the Body and Blood of Christ" (*De Corpore et Sanguine Domini*).

This stirred up a violent controversy, especially among some Benedictine monks. By the middle of the eleventh century, a monk by the name of Berengar (or Berengarius) became the champion of those who denied the Real Presence of Christ in the Eucharist. He was condemned by the Church in A.D. 1050 but refused to retract. So in A.D. 1059 he was ordered to subscribe to a statement drawn up by Pope Nicholas II, which said: "The bread and wine placed on the altar are, after consecration, not only a sacrament, but also the true Body and Blood of our Lord Jesus Christ" (DS 690).

But Berengar still would not give in. Finally, twenty years later, he signed a formal profession of faith approved by Pope Gregory VII at the Sixth Council of Rome in A.D. 1079. This profession of faith is basic to the Catholic Church's teaching on the Real Presence:

> I believe interiorly and profess publicly that the bread and wine, which are placed on the altar, through the mystery of the Sacred Prayer and the words of our Redeemer are substantially changed into the true, proper, and life-giving Flesh and Blood of our Lord Jesus Christ. After the consecration, it is the true Body of Christ, which was born to the Virgin, and which hung on the Cross as an offering for the salvation of the world, and which sits at the right hand of the Father. And it is the true Blood of Christ which was poured forth from His side. And Christ is present not merely by virtue of the sign and power of the Sacrament but in His proper nature and true substance. This I believe, and I will not teach any more against this faith . . . . So help me God and this Holy Gospel of God! (DS 700)

Unfortunately, Berengar relapsed into his previous errors. Yet history tells us that before he died at the age of 88, he was finally reconciled with the Church and repudiated the errors he had been teaching and propagating for more than forty years.

DURANDUS

About one hundred years after Berengar, there arose a cult called the Waldenses. A man named Durandus joined the Church as a convert from the Waldenses. Prior to his conversion, Durandus was very heterodox. The problem was that the Waldenses identified priestly powers with holiness. Once you identify authority in the Church or powers for

conferring the sacraments with sanctity, you break down Christ's institution of the ordained priesthood. Consequently, even though Innocent III
knew that Durandus was a convert to the faith, the pope wanted to make
sure this convert's teaching was orthodox. Consequently, he required
Durandus to sign the following profession of faith in A.D. 1208:

> We, with a sincere heart, firmly and unhesitatingly believe
> and loyally affirm that in the Sacrament of the Eucharist those
> things which before the consecration are bread and wine,
> after the consecration are the true Body and Blood of our
> Lord Jesus Christ. Regarding the Sacrifice, we believe, that a
> good priest does nothing more than this and a bad priest does
> nothing less, because it is not by the merit of the one conse-
> crating that the Sacrifice is accomplished, but by the word of
> the Creator and by the power of the Holy Spirit; consequent-
> ly, we firmly believe and confess, no matter how upright, how
> religious, how holy or how prudent someone may be, he can-
> not and should not consecrate the Eucharist nor perform the
> Sacrifice of the altar unless he is a priest rightly ordained by
> a bishop who can be seen and can be felt and so we firmly
> believe and profess that whoever believes and maintains that
> he can perform the Sacrifice of the Eucharist without previ-
> ously being ordained by a bishop is a heretic. (DS 794)

It is impossible to think of a more timely need for such a profession
of faith in the Holy Eucharist and the priesthood than today. This profession of faith makes clear what today is being so widely challenged.
Only priests can offer Mass. Only priests can change bread and wine
into the living Body and Blood of Christ. Moreover, this profession of
faith teaches it is not the holiness of a person that confers the power
of Eucharistic consecration but rather the sacrament of Holy Orders

conferred on men who are ordained by a bishop who is a successor of the apostles.

JOHN WYCLIFFE

The third major presixteenth-century Eucharistic heresy which provoked a marvelous development of doctrine was led by the priest John Wycliffe. Wycliffe had been a leading scholar at the University of Oxford in England. His teaching had a great influence on John Hus in Bohemia, and Wycliffe is considered one of the major forerunners of Protestantism. He paved the way for the erroneous teaching that hit the Church in the sixteenth century.

Although Wycliffe died in A.D. 1384, his ideas on the Eucharist were not condemned until A.D. 1418 by the general Council of Constance. One reason for the long delay was the rise of the Western Schism during which the unity of the Church was under trial. Prior to this council, errors about the Eucharist spread throughout Christendom, and Wycliffe was one of the leading propagators.

The best way to see what the Church teaches on what happens at Mass is to identify and explain the errors of John Wycliffe. There is a mysterious sense in which we can thank God for drawing so much depth of truth from the errors propagated by those who denied a mystery of the faith. Wycliffe maintained four propositions about the Eucharist, and all four were formally condemned by the Council of Constance. These propositions are:

1. The material substance of bread and the material substance of wine remain in the Sacrament of the Altar.
2. The physical properties of bread and wine do not remain without a substance in the said Sacrament.
3. Christ is not in the Sacrament essentially and really in His own bodily presence.

4. If a bishop or priest is in mortal sin, he does not consecrate (Session 8, 1–4).

It is obvious what Wycliffe denied. It is also clear what the Church in a solemn council affirmed. We can list these affirmations in contra-distinction to Wycliffe's propositions:

1. By the consecration of the Mass, the substance of bread and wine no longer remain on the altar.
2. By the Eucharistic consecration, the species or physical properties of bread and wine remain, but without their substance. The out-ward appearance of bread and wine—color, taste, texture—remain, but not the substance of bread and wine. Under the appearance of bread and wine is Christ's Body and Blood in His humanity, united with His Divinity.
3. By the consecration at Mass, Christ becomes essentially and really present. Essence is what makes a thing what it is; reality is what actually exists and is not a mere figment of the imagination.
4. The sanctity of a priest or bishop does not affect his ability to validly offer Mass or change bread and wine into the living Christ. If he offers Mass in mortal sin, he commits another sin of sacri-lege, but his Mass is valid and Christ is really there.

Whatever else we have learned by now, it ought to be the constancy and stability of Catholic doctrine on the Real Presence. We should also begin to see how any tampering with the Church's Eucharistic doctrine is tampering with the foundations of Catholic Christianity. The Church's strength lies in her consistency of teaching on the Real Presence. Yet as we saw, and will continue to see, this constancy of doctrine in teaching what Christ had revealed at the Last Supper and the never waning faith in the Real Presence is a single principal reason for the stability and unity of the Catholic Church.

P R A Y E R

LORD JESUS, IN THE SIXTEENTH CENTURY YOU ALLOWED THE WORST CALAMITY TO AFFECT YOUR CHURCH IN THE WIDESPREAD DENIAL OF YOUR REAL PRESENCE IN THE HOLY EUCHARIST. GIVE US THE GRACE, WE BEG YOU TO BELIEVE IN YOUR REAL PRESENCE MORE DEEPLY, MORE HEROICALLY THAN WE HAVE EVER DONE SINCE THE DAWN OF CHRISTIANITY. YOU ARE PRESENT AMONG US, THE SAME JESUS WHO WALKED THE STREETS OF PALESTINE AND WAS CRUCIFIED ON CALVARY. YOUR ARE NOW WITH US IN THE BLESSED SACRAMENT. AT HOLY COMMUNION YOU ARE WITHIN US. ALL OF THIS IS THE PRELUDE TO THAT FINAL DAY WHEN WE JOIN YOU IN YOUR HEAVENLY KINGDOM, NEVER AGAIN TO BE SEPARATED FROM YOU IN ALL ETERNITY. AMEN.

4

EUCHARISTIC DOCTRINE IN THE SIXTEENTH CENTURY

It seems only reasonable to devote one whole chapter to the Church's Eucharistic teaching during the sixteenth century. Why is this teaching so important? Because, during the 1500's, a form of Christianity developed that was consciously not Roman Catholic. This form of Christianity withdrew six whole nations from the Catholic Church and has determined the culture of most of North America, including the United States. Moreover, this form of Christianity, on principle, denies that Christ, at the Last Supper, instituted the priesthood and empowered ordained priests to offer the Sacrifice of the Mass—at which bread and wine are changed into the living Flesh and Blood of Christ. Consequently, it is imperative to know what the Catholic Church taught as infallible doctrine during this most divisive era of Christian history.

The main source of information is found in the Council of Trent, which met for eighteen years from 1545 to 1563. During these sessions, the council issued three extensive documents on the Holy Eucharist in this order: on the Real Presence (October 11, 1551), on Holy Communion (July 16, 1562), and on the Sacrifice of the Mass (September 17, 1562). Since our focus here is on the Real Presence, we will concentrate on what the council was called to defend and declare as defined doctrine on the Real Presence of Jesus Christ in the Eucharist. There are five canons specifically defining the Catholic Church's faith in the Real Presence, and each canon is worded in the

25

form of an "anathema." Anathema means accursed. Each canon states: "If anyone says . . . let him be anathema." This means anyone who denies one of these five dogmas is thereby denying a divinely revealed mystery of faith and ceases to be a Catholic.

Looking at each definition in sequence, we will identify each teaching with a title, quote what the Council of Trent defined and briefly explain each definition.

MEANING OF THE REAL PRESENCE

The first definition of the Council of Trent is on the Catholic meaning of the Real Presence. The definition reads: "If anyone says that the Body and Blood together with His whole Divinity of our Lord Jesus Christ and, therefore the whole Christ, is truly, really and substantially contained in the Sacrament of the Most Holy Eucharist, but says that Christ is present in the Sacrament only as in a sign or figure or by His power, let him be anathema" (Session 13, can 1).

There are four key terms in this solemn definition: "the whole Christ," "truly," "really," and "substantially" contained. What are we being taught by these definitions?

We are being told that the Holy Eucharist means "the whole Christ." Everything which belongs to Christ—everything which makes Christ, Christ—is present in the Blessed Sacrament. This consequently means that Christ is present in His divinity as God and in His humanity as man. Christ is present in the Eucharist with His human body and human soul, with His bodily organs and limbs and with His human mind, will and feelings—"the whole Christ." Latin reads *Totus Christus*.

Then we are told Christ is present "truly" and not only symbolically. He is present objectively and not only subjectively in the minds of believers. He is contained in the Blessed Sacrament. Consequently, if our minds realize this objective fact, we possess the truth. There is no more precious truth revealed by Christ than the truth that He is on earth, the whole Christ in the Eucharist.

We are taught that Christ is "really" present and not only figuratively. The Eucharistic presence is not a metaphor or figure of speech. It is reality. Christ exists in the Holy Eucharist. During the century when this Real Presence was defined by the Council of Trent, St. Robert Bellarmine counted the number of meanings given to Christ's words at the Last Supper: "This is My Body. . . .This is My Blood." He found among the Protestant scholars more than two hundred interpretations, except the one which says Christ is "really" present in the Eucharist.

Finally, this definition tells us that Christ is present "substantially" and not merely by the exercise of His power. True, Christ is everywhere exercising His power. Thus, we can legitimately say that Christ is present in every person in the state of grace. Christ confers His grace on those who are in His friendship. But being in the state of grace is not the same as having the Real Presence of Christ in our bodies and souls.

The Real Presence in the Eucharist is absolutely unique. Christ is not present everywhere with the wholeness of His divinity and humanity—only in the Eucharist. In the Eucharist, Christ is present in the *fullness of His being*.

A simple comparison may help to explain what this means. When the angel Gabriel appeared to our Lady at Nazareth and announced to her that she was chosen to become the Mother of the Most High, God as God was present at Nazareth: He was present in the archangel, He was present in our Lady. Otherwise there would have been no Nazareth or Gabriel or Mary. A good definition of nothing is where God is absent. But the moment Mary told the angel, "Be it done unto me according to your word," (Luke 1:38) at that instant God began to be present as the God–man in the womb of His Immaculate Mother. We may therefore literally say that the Holy Eucharist began at the moment of the Incarnation.

It is the second person of the Holy Trinity, which assumed a human nature, which began to be present at the Annunciation, which was born at Bethlehem, died on the cross and rose from the dead on Easter Sunday. It is this Incarnate God who is present in the Holy Eucharist.

There is an analogy which may help explain the distinction. When an American author writes a book that is published worldwide, is he present to those people in Japan who read what he has written? Is his influence present in their hearts and minds? Of course. But unless he flies to Tokyo, he is not "substantially" present to those people.

The Eucharistic Christ is present on earth not only in the sense that He exercises His divine influence on the hearts and minds of human beings. Christ Himself is "substantially" present on earth in the Blessed Sacrament. Only in the Eucharist is Christ present with the wholeness of His divinity and humanity.

That is the first defined dogma on the Real Presence: "the whole Christ" is "truly," "really," and "substantially" contained in the Eucharist.

If the verb "contained" seems strange, it should not be. Why not? Because the physical properties of what had been bread and wine are, as it were, the container which holds the whole Christ within the limits of their physical extension. You might say that Christ is circumscribed within the limits of the accidents or properties of what, before consecration, had been bread and wine.

TRANSUBSTANTIATION

Having defined the existence of Jesus Christ, true God and true man in the Eucharist, the Council of Trent then concentrated on *how* bread and wine are changed into the whole Christ. It had better be changed, otherwise, there is no Real Presence: "If anyone says that the substance of bread and wine remains in the Holy Sacrament of the Eucharist together with the Body and Blood of our Lord Jesus Christ and denies that wonderful and extraordinary change of the whole substance of the wine into His Blood, while only the species of bread and wine remain, a change which the Catholic Church has most fittingly called 'transubstantiation,' let him be anathema" (Sess. 13, can. 2).

As often as we have heard the word "transubstantiation," few Catholics fully know what it means. Transubstantiation means that the substance of bread and wine—what makes them bread and wine—is replaced by the whole Jesus Christ. The "breadness" and "wineness," so to speak, are changed into the living Jesus, true God and true man, whole God and whole man. It does not merely mean that the substance of bread and wine becomes the substance of Christ. The Real Presence is not only the substance of Christ, but the whole of Christ—His substance plus all the human properties of His humanity.

Finally, transubstantiation describes how the physical qualities of bread and wine—their color, texture, taste and whatever else is perceived by the senses—remain, but they lose their substance. The qualities of bread and wine remain, but their substance is replaced by the whole Christ.

We get some idea of how Protestants look upon our faith in transubstantiation by what they write in a standard book titled *Roman Catholicism*. The following quotation is a bit long but deserves to be given to help Catholics know what they are expected to believe about the Real Presence of Christ in the Eucharist.

> The priest supposedly is endowed with power by the bishop at the time of his ordination to change the bread and wine into the literal living body and blood of Christ, which is then known as the "host," and so to bring Him down upon the altar. And that body is said to be complete in all its parts, down to the last eyelash and toenail! How it can exist in thousands of

places and in its full proportions, even in a small piece of bread, is not explained, but is taken on faith as a miracle.

It must not be supposed for a minute that modern Roman Catholics do not literally believe this jumble of medieval superstition. They have been taught it from infancy, and they do believe it. It is the very sternest doctrine of their church. It is one of the chief doctrines, if indeed it is not the chief doctrine, upon which their church rests. The priests preach it literally and emphatically several times a year, and Roman Catholic laymen do not dare express any doubt about it.

After the adoration of the consecrated "host," the uplifted hands of the priest pretend to offer to God the very body and blood of Christ as a Sacrifice for the living and the dead. Then, in the observance of the Eucharist he pretends to eat Him alive, in the presence of the people, also to give Him to the people under the appearance of bread, to be eaten by them.

This doctrine of the mass, of course, is based on the assumption that the words of Christ, "This is My Body." and "This is My Blood." (Matt. 26:26–28), must be taken literally (Lorraine Boettner 175–176).

Since transubstantiation means the Real Presence of Christ, it also means the real absence of bread and wine. To believe this is to be a Roman Catholic.

THE EXTENT OF CHRIST'S PRESENCE

Having defined what takes place in transubstantiation, the Council of Trent identified the extent of this presence. Christ is literally present wherever the physical properties remain of what had been bread and wine. Says Trent, "If anyone denies that in the venerable Sacrament of the Eucharist the whole Christ is contained under each of the species and under every portion of either species when it is divided up, let him be anathema" (Sess. 13, can. 3).

The key word here is "species." The Eucharistic species are the physical properties of what used to be bread and wine before transubstantiation—the species are what is sensibly perceptible in the Holy Eucharist. The species are the size, texture, taste and weight of what was formerly bread and wine.

What does the Church tell us about the species? She infallibly teaches that the entire Christ is entirely present in every particle of the consecrated host and in every drop of what looks and tastes like wine. In the whole Host, Christ is there. Broken in half, Christ is in both parts. Even a single particle contains the whole living Christ. How this needs to be known and believed in our "post-modern" Christian world!

We are also told that the whole Christ is fully and equally present in either species, so we do not have to receive under both forms. A single drop in the chalice after consecration contains the whole Christ.

REAL PRESENCE INDEPENDENT OF COMMUNION

It must seem strange that anyone would come up with the idea that Christ is present only if and when and as long as a person goes to Communion, but once Communion is over, there is no more Real Presence in the Blessed Sacrament. As strange as it may seem, this is exactly what many of the so-called reformers have held. So many people in the sixteenth century said Christ is present only when and if and as long as you are receiving the Holy Eucharist. But the Council of Trent declared: "If anyone says that after the consecration, the Body and Blood of our Lord Jesus Christ are not present in the marvelous Sacrament of the Eucharist, but are present only in the use of the sacrament while it is being received, and not before or after and that the true Body of the Lord does not remain in the consecrated Host or particles that are kept or left over after Communion, anyone who denies that, let him be anathema" (Session 13, can. 4).

If you know what ideas are being circulated today in nominally Catholic quarters, you have no doubt how relevant this cardinal definition is. To deny the doctrine of transubstantiation is only logical for those who have separated from the Catholic Church to either reject the Eucharist entirely, which some do, or keep the word "Eucharist" in name and talk about Christ's Presence only in Communion. But we see what happened and is happening now again to the meaning of Christ's "presence" in the Eucharist once the real meaning of transubstantiation was lost. You may call it the "Lord's Supper." You may call it the "Liturgy." You may call it the "Eucharist." But people no longer speak of a "Real Presence" which does not depend on its being received by the faithful.

I have reasoned with too many priests who are caught up in the miasma that is penetrating the Catholic Church today. I tell them: "Look Father, Christ is present in the Eucharist not only when you or the people receive Communion. He is present in the Eucharist. Period."

A young man recently came to the rostrum after I had given a lecture in Ann Arbor. He told me he was sitting in church during a Mass at which Holy Communion was distributed in the form of leavened bread—which is wrong, but nevertheless, it was consecrated. He watched the people coming up to Communion and noticed the floor was covered with crumbs—not crumbs of bread, but particles of the Sacred Species. He told me, "After everybody left the church, I went over to the sanctuary and began putting the particles into my handkerchief. The pastor saw me from the sacristy and shouted, 'What are you doing?' I told him I was picking up the particles after Holy Communion because I understand each particle is Jesus Christ. The pastor told me 'Get out!'

He saw I did not move, so he pulled me by my collar and dragged me out of the church!"

We had better know—we had better understand—that the Church defined that the whole Christ is present even under a microscopic particle of the consecrated Host. Once we believe that Jesus Christ is truly present in the Holy Eucharist, it is only logical then to respect and adore our Lord, no matter how small the particle or drop from the chalice may be.

EUCHARISTIC ADORATION

This definition comes as no surprise. Once we believe Christ is really present in the Holy Eucharist, it is only logical to conclude that we should worship Him. The last thing we human beings want from another human being is to be ignored. The same is true with Christ present in the Eucharist. So now we look at the definition of the Holy Eucharist as the Adorable Sacrament.

The Council of Trent goes into some detail defining what so desperately needs to be known, publicized and practiced today: "If anyone says that Christ, the only-begotten Son of God, is not to be adored in the Holy Sacrament of the Eucharist with the worship of *latria*, that means the worship only to God, including the external worship, and that therefore the Sacrament is not to be honored with extraordinary festive celebrations, nor carried from place to place in processions, according to the praiseworthy universal rite and custom of the Holy Church or that the Sacrament is not to be publicly exposed for peoples' veneration and to those who adore the Holy Eucharist are idolaters, let him be anathema" (Session 13, can. 4). Human language could not be clearer. Nor could the message be more important.

As our reflections go on, we should have ample opportunity to further explain and expound on the solemn teaching of the Church on the adorableness of Christ present in the Blessed Sacrament. I have been privileged in working for the Holy See for more than thirty years. I know there is one thing the present Holy Father wants: He pleads and begs the bishops of the Catholic Church not only to tolerate but to promote adoration of the Holy Eucharist. I may be bold to say that the future of the Catholic Church depends in large measure on believing Catholics acting on their belief and adoring our Eucharistic Lord. However, it is not only the future of the Church which depends on this mystery of faith being believed, understood and lived out. It is indeed the welfare of the whole world. This I know, because that is my assignment from the Vicar of Christ—to do everything in my power to promote Eucharistic adoration, first among members of the hierarchy, then among priests, and then among all the people of God. It is not only the hope of the Holy Father to restore faith in the Real Presence where it has been removed, but also to strengthen the peoples' faith in the Blessed Sacrament where it is still reserved. Thus, believing in the Real Presence, Catholics will act on what they believe and thereby obtain from Jesus Christ what only He can give—the light and the strength to the spiritually blind and paralyzed human beings of today. This comes from the same Christ who walked the streets of Palestine doing good then. He wants to do good now, but it depends on our faith.

P R A Y E R

LORD JESUS, WE THANK YOU FOR THE CLEAR, UNAMBIGUOUS TEACHING OF YOUR CHURCH ON THE REAL PRESENCE, BUT WE ASK YOU, DEAR LORD, TO OPEN OUR MINDS TO PENETRATE INTO THE MEANING OF THE REALITY WE BELIEVE, SO THAT BELIEVING IN YOU WHOM WE DO NOT SEE WITH OUR BODILY SENSES, WE MAY BEHOLD YOU UNVEILED IN THAT ETERNAL EUCHARIST WHICH IS THE MEANING OF THE BEATIFIC VISION. AMEN.

5

EUCHARISTIC DOCTRINE FROM THE SIXTEENTH CENTURY INTO MODERN TIMES

We have been concentrating on the Church's teaching on the Holy Eucharist, with special emphasis on the Real Presence. Our first reflection focused on the Church's teaching up to the sixteenth century. Then, we looked at what the Church taught about the Eucharist in the sixteenth century itself—by then, the most divisive century of the Church's existence. But we saw how the Council of Trent made it absolutely clear that "the whole Jesus" is "truly," "really," and "substantially" present in the Blessed Sacrament.

Now we turn to the Church's teachings on the Eucharist from the sixteenth century to modern times. Let me point out that one of the marvelous effects of the Council of Trent was to stabilize the Church's magisterial authority in countries that separated from the unity of the Church during the so-called Reformation. The council also strengthened the Church's faith in the Holy Eucharist, with emphasis on the Real Presence. In fact, one of the least publicized results of the Council of Trent was the tremendous growth in Eucharistic devotion on a scale quite unknown in previous centuries. We can call it a renaissance of Eucharistic piety in the Catholic world. In this era, new religious institutes came into existence with the expressed purpose of adoring the Blessed Sacrament and with an apostolate of promoting Eucharistic adoration among the faithful.

However, from the Council of Trent to the Modern Age is a long time. And the evil spirit was active. As always happens when the evil spirit sees the Church flourishing, he redoubles his effort to break down the holiness and fidelity of believing Christians. By the late eighteenth century, throughout the nineteenth century and especially in our own twentieth and twenty-first centuries, forces hostile to Catholic Christianity became more organized, more effective, and more devastating than ever before. I believe these forces can be reduced to two: modernism and secularism.

Our purpose now is not to analyze these alien forces in themselves, but rather to see how the Church, under divine guidance, defended and deepened our understanding of Catholic Eucharistic doctrine as it was being attacked by modernism and secularism. After examining this era, you might agree with me that the twentieth century will go down in history as the time when adoration and worship of our Lord in the Holy Eucharist began a new era in Eucharistic theology and Eucharistic piety.

MODERNISM

We will look first at modernism and Pope St. Pius X. A simple way to describe modernism is to call it "subjective Christianity." Pius X called modernism the collection of all the heresies of Christian history. So it was. At its root, modernism is basing one's faith on one's own inner mind and feelings rather than conforming the mind to God and His objective truth.

With the growth of rationalism in the eighteenth and nineteenth centuries, every mystery of divine revelation soon became subjected to human scrutiny. Every truth of the Christian faith was reduced to each person's private, subjective judgment, such that each person could take an element of the Christian faith and decide for themselves whether it should be fully believed, conditionally accepted or simply rejected.

The law of rationalism put God's revelation at the mercy of man's reason. Rationalism could really be called "reasonism." The final source of so-called "truth" was no longer revelation by God to which the mind conforms, but one's own human reason. Unless, and only insofar as each person could explain a revealed mystery, nothing was to be accepted as true. Man was standing in judgment on God.

As rationalism penetrated into some learned Catholic quarters, it became known as "modernism." Pope St. Pius X realized modernism's threat to the very foundations of Christianity. He also realized that the main target of modernism was the Church's faith in two mysteries: the Incarnation and the Holy Eucharist. That is why in 1907, Pius X condemned a series of modernist errors, especially those regarding the Incarnation and Christ's institution of the Sacraments, including the Holy Eucharist.

Every condemned modernist error had its roots in a reinterpretation of Sacred Scripture. Modernists used *eisegesis* when interpreting Scripture. As explained before, *exegesis* means drawing the truth out of Scripture, whereas *eisegesis* reading into Scripture what is not there. Modernists went back to the Sacred Scriptures and said, "For too long, Christians have taken the Scriptures at face value, naïvely claiming there are no errors in the Bible. And like little children, they have refused to 'de-mythologize' the Scriptures and scrape off the heavy layer of mythology in order to get down to the roots of what the Bible is really teaching."

So what is the New Testament "really teaching," according to the modernists? Whatever the modernist said, whatever they, in their own subjective minds, said was there in the New Testament. God's revelation through Sacred Scripture was put at the mercy of man's reason.

The basic face of modernism condemned by Pius X was the belief that Scriptures are not objective history but the subjective creation of fervent believers who added to the Scriptures and simply projected their own pious imagination about Jesus Christ. Thus, Pius X condemned the following propositions:

1. The divinity of Christ is not proved from the Gospels, but it is a dogma that the Christian consciousness deduced from its notion of the Messiah (cf. *Lamentabili Sane*, 27).
2. It is impossible to reconcile the obvious meaning of the Gospel text with the teaching of our theologians about the consciousness and infallible knowledge of Jesus Christ (cf. 32).

Given these premises, it is no wonder the modernists undermined all the Sacraments and, with special learned virulence, undermined Christ's "alleged" institution of the Holy Eucharist. Along with denying the institution of the Eucharist, they had to logically deny Christ's instituting the priesthood. But Pope Pius X condemned these beliefs as inconsistent with Catholic teaching: "The opinions on the origin of the sacraments which the Fathers of the Council of Trent held are far different from those which are not correctly held by research historians of Christianity" (*Lamentabili Sane*, 39).

I know the lingo of these big Church historians of Christianity. I know the language, and I know where they got their ideas—from their own proud imagination bloated by years of misguided education.

How then did Pius X react to these devastating errors of modernism? He did so in two ways. He identified these errors and declared they were subversive of Catholic Christianity. There is nothing a heretic fears more than to be identified as a heretic.

St. Pius X also reacted to this virus of modernism by promoting devotion to the Holy Eucharist as had never been done before in the Church's history. He realized no human efforts are a match for the demonic forces at work in modernism. Thus, he restored after fifteen hundred years the practice of frequent communion.

In the age of martyrs of the early Church, Christians went to Mass and Holy Communion every day. They felt they had to because at that time to become a Christian was to become a potential martyr. With the

rise of modernism along with atheistic Marxism and agnostic deter-
minism, Pius X foresaw the rise of opposition to the teachings of Christ
with such virulence as the Church had not experienced since Calvary.
Thus, he realized that the dawn of the twentieth century was the dawn
of another age of martyrs. So he restored frequent reception of Holy
Communion, and he gave for all times the interpretation of the invocation in the Lord's Prayer, "Give us this day our daily bread." Pius X said
this invocation mainly means "give us this day our supernatural bread
of the Holy Eucharist to sustain us in our supernatural life."

He also restored the early reception of Holy Communion by children
because he foresaw that children in the twentieth century must be
brought up from childhood to prepare to live a martyr's life and maybe
even die a martyr's death.

It is no coincidence that Pope Pius XII canonized two very young
saints in the Jubilee year of 1950. St. Maria Goretti was declared a martyr saint, although she lived only twelve years; and St. Dominic Savio
who died at the age of fifteen.

Moreover, the twentieth century has had more martyrs who shed their
blood for Christ than all the martyrs of Christianity from Calvary to the
dawn of the twentieth century put together.

Is it any wonder that, for the first time in the Church's history, Pope
John Paul II authorized the reception of Holy Communion twice on the
same day? The only condition is that the second Communion is received
at Mass. The reason is obvious. Ours is *the* Age of Martyrs. If we are to
live a martyr's life and be ready for a martyr's death, we had better be
sustained by the frequent, indeed daily, reception of the Body and Blood
of Jesus Christ in the Holy Eucharist.

We return to St. Pius X, who lived a martyr's life. You do not challenge the learned academic world without paying for it.

Realizing that the Church was entering a new age, a modern age of martyrs, he opened up the practice of Eucharistic Adoration like never before as he restored the practice of adoring the Eucharist in exposition or in the tabernacle. Pope St. Pius X did all this because he understood the necessity of drawing on the supernatural power of Christ present in the Eucharist in order to combat the modernism which had so deeply infiltrated the Church.

SECULARISM

We now focus on secularism and Pope Paul VI. Remember what we have been doing: We have traced the development of Catholic doctrine on the Eucharist, which is mainly occasioned by the rise of one erroneous teaching after another. From Pius X to Paul VI is less than one hundred years. In fact, it is less than two full generations. Since so much happened in this small period of time, we need to look closely at the marvelous development of Eucharistic doctrine in this era, which has been occasioned by the phenomenal growth of secularism in the modern world. Secularism is a faith believing that only the *saeculum*—this world of space and time—exists. Only this world matters. The growth of secularism in our day has no counterpart in world history. Entire nations, especially the materially developed countries, have made "this worldly" values the norm in their culture. That is why children—unborn children—are being murdered on a scale never before known since the dawn of man's existence. As a result, the Church herself has been deeply affected, and the future of Catholicism in more than one country is in jeopardy.

What is the remedy? Pope Paul VI realized that secularism within the Catholic Church cannot be overcome by mortal efforts but only by drawing on the power of the God who became man to work moral miracles. The Pope realized that God is still on earth in the Blessed Sacrament of the altar.

He spent his Pontificate pointing out, urging and stressing the Real Presence of Christ in the Eucharist. He published the only papal encyclical exclusively devoted to defending the Real Presence. In the encyclical *Mysterium Fidei* (Mystery of Faith), Pope Paul VI urged the Catholic faithful to worship our Lord in the Blessed Sacrament as their principal source of life and strength on earth to cope with the demonic powers of secularism unleashed in our day.

How did Paul VI promote worship of our Lord in the Eucharist? Of course, through the Sacrifice of the Mass and by receiving Communion, but he also did so in a way that no pope in history made so plain with emphasis: through devotion to Christ's Real Presence in the Blessed Sacrament.

This devotion to the Blessed Sacrament is a key part of two documents by Paul VI that go together: *Mysterium Fidei* (1965) and *Humanae Vitae* (1968). In *Humanae Vitae*, the use of contraception was condemned. Yet, secularism had so deeply infected the prosperous and educated countries that before the end of 1968, bishops in one country after another held emergency conferences: "How are we going to cope with *Humanae Vitae*?" Sadly, in one nation after another, their Excellencies left the practice of contraception to the consciences of each individual Catholic. But of course, even without the Church's magisterial infallible teaching, contraception has always been a grave sin of the moral law. *Humanae Vitae* simply recalled the Catholic world to the basic moral principles in the practice of chastity. In *Humanae Vitae*, Paul VI pointed out that the virtue of chastity must be practiced if marriage and the family, as well as the priesthood and religious life, are even to survive.

But how can we remain chaste in a sex-mad world? We can ask: How, dear God, can the world (beginning with the Catholic world) protect itself from the inroads of secularism in the moral order? From whom can we get the strength to maintain ourselves in chastity before marriage, in marriage or in the priesthood and religious life? Where can we get the strength? In *Mysterium Fidei*, Paul VI gives us the answer: "Only from Jesus Christ who is on earth to provide us with the miraculous power we need to remain pure in His eyes so we may be chaste in our lives" (66). Approaching Christ in the Eucharist, we can be successful in begging for the strength this world needs to come back to its chaste common sense, and thus, in God's providence, be saved.

I recommend all of you to read *Mysterium Fidei*. In one paragraph after another, the Pope emphasized the need for Catholics not only to assist and participate in the Sacrifice of the Mass and receive Holy Communion frequently or daily. The Pope also emphasized the daily practice of worshipping our Lord in the Holy Eucharist by adoring Him and evoking His help. While reminding the Catholic world of the foundational faith of Christianity in the Real Presence, he quoted the entire profession of faith of Berengarius, whom we remember from our earlier reflection. Having then spelled out that "Jesus Christ is on earth," the Pope went on to tell everyone—bishops, priests and religious; the married and the single; the young and the old—to cultivate as they had never done before a greater devotion to the Holy Eucharist, either the Eucharist exposed on the altar or reserved in the tabernacles of all the Catholic churches around the world.

This had never been done at such length and with such depth and clarity by any sovereign Pontiff in Catholic history. The Pope knew so well that no one but Jesus Christ—the miracle worker of Palestine then and the miracle worker on earth today—can overcome the powers of evil that have been unleashed by the powers of hell in today's world.

Addressing the bishops directly, the Pope reminds them that the Eucharist is to be reserved in churches and oratories. Our Lord in the Blessed Sacrament should be the center of every parish and the epicenter of every religious community. Indeed, the Eucharist is to be the center of the Universal Church and of all humanity. Why? As Paul VI says, "Because beneath the veil of the Eucharistic elements is contained the Invisible Head of the Church, the Redeemer of the world, the center of all hearts, through whom all things are and through whom we exist" (68). Never before have we had such need of invigorating our faith in the Real Presence and putting that faith into practice. Only Christ on earth can overcome the powers of evil that God in His mysterious providence has allowed to penetrate our day.

The phenomenal growth of Eucharistic devotion and worship in the Catholic Church stands to reason—reason enlightened by faith. Once we realize who is on earth—no less than He was in first-century Asia Minor—it is no wonder that those who believe will flock to be in His presence, to honor and thank Him as their God, with weeping emphasis to beg Him for the graces they so desperately need today.

Experience has shown that as a parish or a diocese or a country or religious institute grows, it is due mainly to the worship of Christ in the Holy Eucharist. As a bishop in Ireland told me, "We have had more vocations than ever before in modern history in those dioceses and from those parishes where the Holy Eucharist is exposed and worshiped, even day and night by the faithful."

You might say, "Of course!" It is the same Jesus who promised to work miracles. Even greater miracles, the Vicar of Christ tells us, through the Blessed Sacrament. But on one condition: provided we believe.

PRAYER

LORD JESUS, YOU INSTITUTED THE HOLY EUCHARIST TO BE OUR CONSTANT COMPANION ALL THROUGH LIFE. YOU GAVE US THE BLESSED SACRAMENT IN ORDER TO BE WITH US, DAY AND NIGHT, UNTIL THE DAWN OF ETERNITY. WE BELIEVE THE HOLY EUCHARIST IS YOURSELF, PRESENT AMONG US JUST AS TRULY AS YOU WERE PRESENT AMONG YOUR DISCIPLES IN THE FIRST CENTURY OF CHRISTIANITY. DEEPEN OUR FAITH IN YOUR REAL PRESENCE NOW ON EARTH, HIDDEN IN THE HOLY EUCHARIST, AS A PRELUDE TO THAT EVERLASTING EUCHARIST WHEN YOU WILL BE WITH US FOR ALL ETERNITY. DEEPEN OUR FAITH IN YOUR EUCHARISTIC PRESENCE IN OUR MIDST. STRENGTHEN OUR TRUST IN YOU. ABOVE ALL, DEEPEN OUR LOVE FOR YOU HIDDEN IN THE BLESSED SACRAMENT, UNTIL WE SEE YOU FACE TO FACE IN THAT EVERLASTING DAY FOR WHICH WE WERE MADE. AMEN.

6

The Sacrament of the Eucharist

In our previous reflections, we looked at the Church's teaching on the Real Presence of Christ in the Eucharist. We have seen how the Church has grown in her understanding of the Eucharist as she defended the integrity of the Real Presence from various erroneous teachings that arose throughout the centuries.

Now we will examine more clearly what we believe when we say the Holy Eucharist is a sacrament. Why is this important? Because we know the Eucharist is one of the seven sacraments instituted by Christ. We also know the Eucharist is commonly called the "Blessed Sacrament" or the "Sacrament of the Altar." However, using beautiful words like these is not enough. We need to clearly understand what these words mean. More specifically, we need to grasp what we mean when we speak of the Eucharist as a sacrament.

To guide us through this reflective meditation, we will address three questions: *What* is a sacrament? *How* is the Holy Eucharist a sacrament? And, *why* is the Holy Eucharist a sacrament?

WHAT IS A SACRAMENT?

Before we can understand what the sacraments are, we must first realize there are two levels of life that God has offered the human race. There is the natural life, which we have as human beings. It is called natural because we are conceived and born with this life. At the moment of conception, God creates our immortal soul which He infuses into a body provided by our parents. Our bodies are destined to die when the principle of our natural life, the soul, separates from the body.

But there is also the supernatural life, which we receive at Baptism. It is called supernatural because it is not natural, but above (*super*) our created nature as human beings. This supernatural life is the indwelling of the Holy Spirit, who produces sanctifying grace in our souls. Having this life of God in our souls entitles us to the beatific vision of God in a heavenly eternity.

What then are the sacraments? Instituted by Christ, the sacraments are sensibly perceptible signs by which He communicates His divine grace and inward sanctification to our souls. Sacraments are the means Christ instituted to:

1. Give us supernatural life in Baptism.
2. Strengthen this supernatural life through Confirmation.
3. Nourish this supernatural life through the Eucharist.
4. Restore and/or heal this supernatural life through Penance or Confession.
5. Prepare us for eternity by readying our supernatural life for heaven through Anointing of the Sick.
6. Empower those who have a vocation to confer, restore or strengthen the supernatural life in others through Holy Orders.
7. Strengthen those who are so prepared by God to cooperate with a married spouse in growing in the supernatural life and sharing this life with the children God may wish to send them through Marriage.

The sacraments of the New Law have three essential elements: They were instituted by Christ during His visible stay on earth; they are sensibly perceptible rites; and, they actually confer the supernatural grace they signify.

HOW IS THE HOLY EUCHARIST A SACRAMENT?

With this background, we are ready to ask ourselves, "How is the Eucharist a sacrament?" We answer: The Eucharist is not only *a* sacrament. It is *the* sacrament—the greatest of all sacraments. The goal and purpose of all the other sacraments is to lead to a deeper union with Christ in the Eucharist.

More still, if every sacrament is a channel of grace, the Eucharist is a channel for more grace. The Eucharist is nothing less than the Author of grace. Jesus Christ, the Son of God, became man in order to restore to us the life of grace that humanity lost through sin. Christ became man to communicate through His humanity the grace which He possessed in its totality.

If Catholics were asked to name the seven sacraments, many would of course include the Eucharist. If they were further asked to describe the sacrament of the Eucharist, they would probably answer, "The sacrament of the Eucharist is Holy Communion." This answer is correct, but it is inadequate. The Holy Eucharist *is* Jesus Christ, the source of all grace.

We have already spoken about development of doctrine in the Catholic Church's teaching. Among the areas of doctrinal development is the Church's deepening realization that while the Holy Eucharist is indeed one sacrament, this one sacrament confers grace in three different ways:

1. As the Sacrifice of the Mass, the Eucharist is the Sacrifice Sacrament.
2. As Holy Communion, the Eucharist is the Communion Sacrament.
3. As the Real Presence, the Eucharist is the Presence Sacrament.

In the next three chapters, we shall look more closely at the Holy Eucharist as a sacrament in each of these three ways. For the present, we want to make sure that we recognize how the Eucharist is a sacrament—

and therefore a channel of grace—on three levels: as Sacrifice, as Communion and as Presence.

WHY IS THE HOLY EUCHARIST A SACRAMENT?

Even as we ask this question, we should wonder why we need to ask it. Once we realize not *what* the Eucharist is, but *who* the Eucharist is, it seems almost trivial, not to say profane, to ask why the Eucharist is a sacrament.

Why is the Eucharist a sacrament? Because Jesus is *the* Sacrament of the New Law. He *is the* Second Person of the Trinity who became Incarnate. He is the paramount, principal, primary and providential channel of grace to the human race. Once we realize that the Eucharist *is* Jesus Christ, a better question would be, How could the Eucharist *not* be a channel of grace? If we say the Eucharist is not a sacrament, then we would have to say that Christ is not a sacrament. But then there would be no channels of grace at all. We would be living in a dream world of the spirit. We would be denying that the source of all grace is Jesus Christ Himself, who is really present in the Eucharist.

That is why it is impossible to grasp too clearly the truth of Catholic Christianity in regard to the powers of the priesthood which Christ conferred on the apostles and enabled them to pass on through ordination.

It is impossible to see too clearly that through the powers of the priesthood, we have Jesus Christ with us, among us, near us and constantly available to us. Why is He with us? So that by believing in His Eucharistic Presence now on earth, we might come to Him—as He has come to us—and obtain from Him the supernatural graces we so desperately need for ourselves, for those dear to us and for the whole world.

I can think of no better way to conclude this chapter than by quoting from St. Alphonsus Liguori, founder of the Redemptorists and patron of confessors and spiritual directors.

—————— P R A Y E R ——————

"Our Holy Faith teaches us, and we are bound to believe, that in the consecrated Host, Jesus Christ is really present under the species of bread. But we must also understand that He is thus present on our altars, as on the throne of love and mercy, to dispose graces and then to show us the love He bears us by being pleased to dwell night and day in the midst of us." Amen. (H.E. p. 113).

7

THE SACRIFICE SACRAMENT OF
THE HOLY EUCHARIST

The purpose of this chapter is to explain how the Mass is the Sacrifice Sacrament of the Eucharist. Again, we will draw on the Church's teaching, especially focusing on definitions from the Council of Trent in the sixteenth century. We will also examine the writings of Pope Pius XII on which the Second Vatican Council mainly built its historic document on the Eucharistic Liturgy.

THE COUNCIL OF TRENT AND THE MASS

We have been drawing on the Church's teaching at Trent. Why? Mainly because during the sixteenth century, every Catholic doctrine on the Eucharist was not only questioned or challenged but openly denied. Trent synthesized all the Eucharistic doctrine of the Catholic Church in the first fifteen centuries of her history. But more than that, Trent sharpened and clarified this doctrine under the pressure of the most widespread errors on the Eucharist in the Church's previous fifteen hundred years.

If there was one dominant feature in the writings of Luther, Calvin and Zwingli in their break with the Roman Catholic Church, it was their claim that Christ never instituted the sacrament of Holy Orders, which empowers ordained priests to consecrate bread and wine into the Body and Blood of Christ during the Sacrifice of the Mass.

With this in mind, we understand why the Council of Trent published nine lengthy formal "anathemas" condemning anyone who held certain erroneous positions on the Sacrifice of the Mass. Each Tridentine declaration begins with the familiar "If anyone says . . . " and concludes with "Let him be anathema,"—let him be condemned. Three of these nine definitions are especially pertinent to our subject and should be quoted and explained:

1. "If anyone says that in the Mass, a true and proper Sacrifice is not offered to God or that the sacrificial offering consists merely in the fact that Christ is given to us to eat, let him be anathema."
2. "If anyone says that by the words 'Do this in commemoration of me' Christ did not make the apostles priests or that He did not command that they and other priests should offer His Body and Blood, let him be anathema."
3. "If anyone says that the Sacrifice of the Mass is merely an offering of prayers and of thanksgiving or that it is a simple memorial of the Sacrifice offered on the Cross and not propitiatory or that it benefits only those who communicate and the Mass should not be offered for the living and the dead for sins, punishment, satisfaction and other necessities, let him be anathema" (Session 22, cans. 1–3).

Unfortunately, every one of these anathemized statements is now being circulated and published and taught widely in nominally Catholic circles today. If you look at weekly parish bulletins from some dioceses, you will notice that so few refer to the Sacrifice of the Mass as a Sacrifice or even Mass anymore. It is called a "Liturgy" or "Eucharist." But let it be known: No one can be Catholic without believing Christ instituted the Sacrifice of the Mass.

So what is the Council of Trent telling us about the Mass as a true Sacrifice? In the Mass, the same Christ, who offered Himself on Calvary, now offers Himself in an unbloody manner on the altar.

Moreover, the Mass is a true Sacrifice because it is the same Jesus really present on the altar through the words of consecration. In the Mass, we have the same priest, Christ, who offers the same Victim, Christ. Christ offers Himself.

Then, at the Last Supper, Christ ordained His apostles as priests when He told them, "Do this in commemoration of Me." What had Christ done? He changed bread and wine into His own living person and He offered His Flesh and Blood to the heavenly Father for the redemption of a sinful human race.

Again, Trent tells us that the Sacrifice of the Mass is not only a liturgical ceremony nor merely a celebration or remembrance of the Sacrifice on Calvary. No, the Mass *is* a Sacrifice. In fact, the Mass is *the* Sacrifice, which St. Paul tells us wiped out all the other sacrifices that had been offered until the coming of Christ. Christ's death on the Cross objectively merited the graces to redeem the world, but Christ must now subjectively communicate these graces to us. The Sacrifice of the Mass is the principal means by which those graces are channeled to a sin-laden world. We believe the Sacrifice on that first Good Friday is re-enacted or re-presented in the Eucharistic Sacrifice of the Mass. Christ's Blood was shed only once—physically. He died only once, but He dies mystically and spiritually every time Mass is offered. After all, Christ in the Mass has the same free will by which He chose to die on Calvary. The essence of sacrifice is the *voluntary* surrender of something precious to God.

Moreover, for our purpose, the Mass is a sacrament which confers numerous graces on the whole human family. What kind of graces does the Sacrifice Sacrament of the Eucharist confer?

- The grace of propitiation or expiation for sin. Propitiation means obtaining graces from God that will make up for, amend and expiate the ravages of sin.

- The grace of obtaining mercy from God, who removes more or less of the guilt incurred by our sins. We may say that guilt is the loss of divine grace.

Siegmund Freud was not only not a Christian, he was not even a believer in a personal God. Yet after a lifetime of clinical practice, Freud said he had yet to meet a single client who was not troubled by the sense of guilt. Guilt is the foundation of all psychological disorders, so we had better know what guilt is. Guilt is the loss of grace. The Sacrifice Sacrament of the Eucharist restores more or less of that lost grace.

- The grace of repentance and true interior sorrow for our having offended a just God.
- The grace of remission of the sufferings that are due to us because we have sinned.
- The grace enlightening our minds which have been darkened by sin. Sin and darkness go together throughout the Bible and throughout human history. Two millennia of Christian history teach us that the most irrational idiots are those who may have a superb intellect but are steeped in sin.
- The grace of strengthening our wills to do good and avoid evil, because our own wills have been weakened by sins.
- The grace of obtaining grace for others, especially conversion for hardened sinners and acceptance of the true faith for those who may never have even heard the Gospel preached to them.
- The grace of inspiring and enabling us to make sacrifices out of love for God. How generous can we be? The most demanding sacrifice we can make is to surrender the most precious creature who happens to have our name. How we love that creature and do not want to give it up! But we can do so through the strength received from the Sacrifice Sacrament of the Eucharist.

Is it any wonder that over the centuries the saints have urged the faithful to assist at Mass as often as possible?

POPE PIUS XII AND THE SACRIFICE OF THE MASS

Why of all Pontiffs should we choose Pius XII? Because during his Pontificate, he wrote extensively on the Sacrifice of the Mass, and he laid the groundwork for the authentic teaching of Vatican II.

Similar to the sixteenth century, many nominal Catholics in the twentieth and twenty-first centuries have either abandoned their faith entirely or are struggling to remain believing Catholics. Pius XII repeatedly declared that Catholics in this century need to deepen their understanding of the Mass or they risk losing their faith in how indispensable the Mass is for their eternal salvation. Pius XII warned that the modern Western world must rediscover the indispensability of the Sacrifice Sacrament of the Eucharist. Otherwise the Church will not survive in those cultures, or even in whole continents.

With this theme for his pontificate, Pius XII on November 20, 1947, published the historic document, *Mediator Dei*, better known in English as *The Sacred Liturgy*. In more than thirty thousand words, he explained how the Sacrifice of the Mass is absolutely necessary for our salvation. It is the sacrament through which Christ dispenses the graces He won for us on Calvary. Certainly Christ died on the Cross for the redemption of the world. He gained all the supernatural light and strength we need to reach our heavenly destiny. But we must have access to this supernatural treasury. The principal conduit for these divine blessings is the Sacrifice Sacrament of the Eucharist.

The Pope said: "Christ built on Calvary a purifying and saving reservoir which He filled with the Blood He poured forth. But if men do not immerse themselves in its waves and do not therefore cleanse themselves of the stains of their sins, they certainly cannot be saved" (77).

So when we say the Mass is a sacrament, it means graces are conferred just because Mass is being offered. Thus, we should make sure that every priest we know offers Mass every day!

These graces are especially those that have to do with sin and the remission of both guilt (loss of grace) and punishment for sins. Because the Mass is a sacrament, it confers these graces infallibly. It confers these graces for the whole human race, dependent on the degree of faith a person has and on the moral disposition of the individual.

However, it is not enough to believe intellectually in the Mass. It is not enough to attend Mass or even participate in the Mass. The key to unlocking the treasures of Calvary is to live the Mass. We benefit only as much from the graces of the Sacrament of the Mass as we are living the images of Jesus Christ, whose life on earth was one long Sacrifice, in the total surrender of His human will to the divine will of His Father.

P R A Y E R

LORD JESUS, WE BELIEVE YOU INSTITUTED THE SACRIFICE SACRAMENT OF THE MASS AS THE PRINCIPAL SOURCE OF GRACE FOR A SIN-LADEN HUMAN RACE. OPEN OUR MINDS TO SEE WITH THE EYES OF FAITH THAT IN EVERY MASS, YOU ARE OFFERING YOURSELF OVER AND OVER AGAIN TO YOUR HEAVENLY FATHER. YOU CAN NO LONGER DIE, BUT DEAR JESUS, WE CAN. HELP US TO DIE, DIE TO OURSELVES, SO THAT WE MAY COOPERATE WITH THE OCEAN OF BLESSINGS THAT YOU ARE POURING OUT FROM THE SACRIFICE OF THE MASS OFFERED THROUGHOUT THE WORLD. WE PRAY THAT BY LIVING THE MASS HERE ON EARTH WE MAY ENTER THE HEAVENLY GLORY YOU WON FOR US WHEN YOU WERE CRUCIFIED ON GOOD FRIDAY. AMEN.

8

THE EUCHARIST AS COMMUNION SACRAMENT

There is generally no difficulty speaking about the Holy Eucharist as Communion Sacrament. In fact, this is the most common way most Catholics think of the Holy Eucharist. However, our perspective will be more specific. We will reflect on the meaning of the Holy Eucharist as a channel of grace and on how Holy Communion is a means of obtaining supernatural sustenance for the divine life we received at baptism.

The Church's doctrinal history of Holy Communion goes back to the first century as found in the *Didache*, the teaching of the twelve Apostles, written around the year A.D. 90. From then on, there has been a steady stream of ecclesiastical teaching which continues to our day. As might be expected, this teaching has grown in depth and clarity due to the challenges of erroneous doctrine, so by now, we can speak without ambiguity about the sacramental effects of receiving our Lord in Holy Communion.

SOURCE OF THE CHURCH'S TEACHING

The primary source of our faith in the effects of Holy Communion is the clear teaching of Christ Himself as recorded by the evangelist St. John. As we have already seen, heretical sects arose before the second century claiming that Christ was not truly God nor truly man. That is why, as history tells us, St. John was inspired by the Holy Spirit to write the fourth Gospel—mainly to show that Jesus was indeed both true God and true man. That is why John concentrates so much on showing that Jesus was God Himself in human form. That is also why St. John devotes the whole sixth chapter of his Gospel (72 verses) to the account of Christ's promise to give us His Flesh to eat and His Blood to drink. Just as uncompromisingly as Christ taught that He was giving His real Body and His real Blood for our spiritual nourishment, so the Catholic Church has taught ever since.

From the dawn of Christianity, the Church understood Holy Communion to be the reception of the living Christ Himself. But now, there has been such a medley of erroneous ideas about the Eucharist as communion that we had better make sure we know what we mean by Holy Communion. We believe that Holy Communion *is* Jesus Christ, in the fullness of His divinity and humanity, whom we receive into our bodies in order to sanctify our souls.

STATE OF GRACE REQUIRED

When we say Holy Communion confers grace, this does not mean it confers sanctifying grace to those who are not already in the state of grace. On the contrary, Holy Communion is a sacrament of the living. In order to receive faithfully, a person must first of all be living in friendship with God—living in the state of grace. Otherwise, so far from benefiting from Holy Communion, a person commits a sacrilege. And in St. Paul's words, such a person "draws condemnation on himself" (1 Cor. 11:29).

I am no mystic who can read the hearts of human beings, but we do not have to be mystics to know that a lot of people, especially in our country, are receiving sacrilegious Communions. With a horrendous drop in the amount of people frequenting confession, common sense tells us many people with mortal sins are still going to Communion. But as St. Paul tells us, this Communion brings their own condemnation.

This follows logically from Christ's own teaching that Holy Communion nourishes the life of God already possessed by the Communicant. We do not feed a dead body with natural food and drink.

No less can we feed a spiritually dead soul with supernatural food and drink. The sacrament Christ instituted to restore supernatural life to a person in mortal sin is the Sacrament of Penance, not the Sacrament of Holy Communion.

The flood of errors rampant in allegedly Catholic circles is a deluge. I was recently shown a parish bulletin in which parishioners were instructed to tell only one sin when they go to confession. What if I have committed two mortal sins? How could I revitalize my spiritual life in order to receive Holy Communion faithfully?

EFFECTS OF THE SACRAMENT OF COMMUNION

There are nine effects of Holy Communion which are produced in the person who receives our Lord in the state of grace. Each of these effects has a mounting library of literature explaining what the effects mean and how they sanctify those who receive our Lord worthily. We will just cover these nine effects briefly:

1. Sustenance of Supernatural Life

Following the promise of Christ, the most basic consequence of Holy Communion is to enable the Communicant to remain supernaturally alive. Not once, but several times in the Gospel of John, Jesus came back to this theme: "If anyone eats of this bread, he shall live forever." Again: "Unless you eat the Flesh of the Son of man and drink His Blood, you shall not have life in you." Still again: "He who eats My Flesh and drinks My Blood has life everlasting." And once more: "As the living Father has sent me, and as I live because of the Father, so he who eats Me, he also shall live because of Me" (John 6:52–59).

2. Promise of Bodily Resurrection from the Dead

In the same context of John's Gospel, Christ promised the person receiving Him in Holy Communion: "I will raise him up on the last day"

(John 6:40). Consequently, receiving the glorified Christ into our pathetically mortal bodies is a prelude and promise for having our bodies immortalized and glorified on the day of resurrection at the end of time.

3. Remission of Venial Sins

As explained by the Church, whatever the soul loses by venial sins can be totally restored through Holy Communion. Thus, we can follow through on the same analogy as bodily sustenance. The daily "wear and tear" on our bodies resulting from effort, exertion and fatigue has its spiritual counterpart in the human soul. There are strong, healthy bodies and strong, healthy souls. And there are weak, debilitated human bodies that need repair just as there are weak debilitated human souls in need of repair. In the words of St. Ambrose, "This daily bread (of Holy Communion) is taken as a remedy for daily infirmity."

4. Protection against Future Sins

Two basic forms of spiritual protection are taught by the Church. Holy Communion protects the recipient from the contagion of sin like a "spiritual vaccine." It protects the soul from the assaults of temptation like a supernatural armor against the attacks of the world and the devil.

St. Cyprian, writing in the early third century, says Christians imprisoned and tortured for the name of Christ received from the hand of the bishop the sacrament of the Body and Blood of the Lord, so they would not yield to a Roman prosecutor and deny the faith. Before going on trial, they pleaded, "give me Communion, so I will be able to resist."

From the very beginning of the Church, this was the reason Holy Communion was brought to the early Christians in prisons—for their faith and to strengthen them in their struggle with the enemies of Christ's name. If you think for a moment that the age of persecution has passed, you are living in a dream world. The real world in which we live is a world that hates Christ and His followers. And yes, the verb is "hates." Anytime I begin to doubt that, all I have to do is turn to the media, which will do anything to tear down the name of Christianity and especially loves to humiliate the Catholic Church. Leave it to the media; they do not miss a single opportunity. We desperately need to receive Holy Communion as often as we can to protect us against the virulent hatred found in Christ's enemies today.

5. Curbs the Urges of Concupiscence

We know that concupiscence is the wound of original sin. Concupiscence is the unruly desires of the will and the body which require supernatural control. There is no way known to God or man that we can control our passions of flesh or soul by ourselves or even with the help of other human beings. For years I have told my students in teaching comparative religion that Christianity, with emphasis on Catholic Christianity, must be the one true religion. It provides the control for human beings that we need to live as human beings by controlling ourselves.

If we rely on our own human nature, we simply cannot control our passions of flesh or soul. We need to use supernatural means, especially those found in the Eucharist. This is so true and the verdict of history is certain: either a person receives Holy Communion frequently or regularly or human nature is no match for the passions of the flesh and spirit that plague every human being.

More than fifty years in the priesthood has taught me many things, but this stands out: No one can control their passions on their own. This is especially true for the two most demanding passions of pride and lust—pride to dominate others and lust to enjoy pleasures of the flesh. Either we receive Holy Communion and acquire mastery of these irrational drives, or we become further moral casualties in the war between ourselves and the forces of evil. The greatest saints were among the most passionate people known in human history. But they needed the means of controlling and actually stilling this passionate machine going at ninety miles an hour. They found the supernatural means to do this in the Eucharist.

6. Spiritual Joy

The Church compares the effects of savory food and drink for the body with a spiritual satisfaction assured the soul through Holy Communion. For example, we can eat food A and we can eat food B, and both foods may nourish the body equally. But there is a great difference between eating food you enjoy and eating food with which you have to make an act of faith that it is good for you!

Similarly, we are not only to practice virtue; we are to *enjoy* doing the will of God. Of course, this happiness may be joined with physical or emotional pain. But even so, our living the life of grace should be peace-giving, joy-receiving and happiness-producing. Faith tells us that the principal source of this earthly beatitude is the frequent reception of Holy Communion. For example, people often tell me, "Father, I am trying to do God's will, but it is such a burden. I read the lives of the saints, and I cannot believe it; it must be spiritual fiction. I cannot live a life like that."

In turn, I ask, "How often do you go to Communion?"

"Every week."

"Start going at least twice a week or even every day if you can. Then come back and talk to me again."

Having a doctorate, not in medicine, but in theology, I know one way a doctor recognizes the value of the medication he prescribes: he asks, "Does it do any good?" With fifty years of experience in the priesthood, I can tell you this works. This "prescription"—frequent reception of Holy Communion—truly works.

7. Perseverance in Grace

One of the most sobering truths of our faith is that even a lifetime of virtue is not of itself a guarantee of final perseverance. Final perseverance is a special gift from God that we cannot directly merit as a reward for a lifetime of service to God. Indeed, with a lifetime of struggling and laboring to do the will of God, we might think: "The least God can give me is the guarantee that I am going to die in His friendship." No. I must obtain that gift of final perseverance, the most important grace which will open the doors of heaven.

Final perseverance must be prayed for. That is why we close every Hail Mary with the invocation, "pray for us sinners now and at the hour of our death." We can obtain the grace of final perseverance. The Church tells us the single most powerful guarantee for assurance of dying in God's friendship is frequent and fervent reception of Holy Communion.

8. Growth in the Supernatural Life

It stands to revealed reason that Holy Communion increases sanctifying grace, nurtures our spiritual life and enables us to grow in God's grace as no other means available to us in this valley of tears. There is more here than meets the eye. Every worthy reception of Holy Communion deepens the life of God in our souls, draws us closer to the Holy Trinity and makes us more pleasing to the Divine Majesty. After all, this is the source of growth in the spiritual life. The essence of holiness is not in the practice of virtue but in the person's possession of grace. A newborn child just baptized is holy because that child possesses the grace of God. That is why over the centuries the Communion Sacrament of the Eucharist has been called "Holy Communion." It should really be called "Holifying Communion" or "Sanctifying Communion." The Holy Eucharist sanctifies. The Holy Eucharist makes us more like Christ and increases the divine life in our souls.

9. Remission of Sin

It is part of Christ's teaching that Holy Communion removes both the guilt of venial sin and the debt of pain due to our forgiven sins. This does not minimize the importance and value of the Sacrament of Confession, but it does mean in Holy Communion we have a divinely ordained means for the remission of sin on these two levels: on the remission of guilt of venial sin (not mortal sin) and on the remission of temporal punishment (not eternal punishment) for those sins. Through Holy Communion, our duty to suffer is mitigated by the merciful God. In Holy Communion, we receive the merciful God who exercises His mercy every time we receive His Body into our body, His Soul into our soul. As a result, He makes us less sinful with every Communion we receive. You might say this is the parallel to growth in sanctity.

I would like to close this meditation with the prayer of Thomas Aquinas for thanksgiving after Holy Communion.

PRAYER

"I GIVE YOU THANKS, HOLY LORD, FATHER ALMIGHTY, EVERLASTING GOD, THAT YOU HAVE VOUCHSAFED TO FEED ME, A SINNER, YOUR UNWORTHY SERVANT FOR NO MERITS OF MY OWN, BUT ONLY THROUGH THE GOODNESS OF YOUR GREAT MERCY WITH THE PRECIOUS BODY AND BLOOD OF YOUR SON, OUR LORD JESUS CHRIST. I ASK THAT THIS HOLY COMMUNION MAY NOT ADD TO MY GUILT FOR PUNISHMENT, BUT BECOME A SAVING INTERCESSION FOR PARDON. MAY IT SERVE AS AN ARMOR OF FAITH AND A SHIELD OF GOOD WILL. MAY IT DRIVE OUT MY EVIL INCLINATIONS, DISPEL ALL WICKED DESIRES AND FLESHLY TEMPTATIONS, INCREASE MY CHARITY, PATIENCE, HUMILITY, OBEDIENCE IN ALL MY VIRTUES. MAY IT BE A FIRM DEFENSE AGAINST THE PLOTS OF ALL MY ENEMIES, BOTH SEEN AND UNSEEN; A PERFECT QUIETING OF ALL MOVEMENTS TO SIN BOTH IN MY FLESH AND SPIRIT; A STRONG ATTACHMENT TO YOU, THE ONLY TRUE GOD; AND A HAPPY ENDING OF MY LIFE. I BEG OF YOU TO TEND TO BRING ME, A SINNER, TO THE INEFFABLE FACE WHERE WE WILL, WITH YOUR SON AND THE HOLY SPIRIT WHO ARE TWO HOLY ONES, TWO ALIKE, FULL SATISFACTION, EVERLASTING JOY . . . . MY PLEASURE AND PERFECT HAPPINESS. AMEN." (GRATIAS TIBI AGO DOMINE).

9

The Holy Eucharist as Presence Sacrament

Now we enter directly into the heart of this Eucharistic book. Our aim here is to better understand what we mean when we say the Holy Eucharist is not only the Sacrifice Sacrament of the Mass or the Communion Sacrament, but the Presence Sacrament. When we speak of "Presence Sacrament," we are saying the Real Presence of Christ on earth in the Eucharist is the source of grace four times over:

1. Grace of Realization

This Presence gives a prior grace to those who believe that to come to Jesus Christ in the Eucharist is to adore Him, thank Him, beg for His mercy and ask Him for what they need.

2. Emanating Grace

This Presence is the fountain of divine blessings which Christ pours out to the whole world just because He, the Son of God in human form, is on earth in the Blessed Sacrament.

3. Actual Grace for Ourselves

This Presence is a source of actual graces (illuminations of the mind and inspirations of the will) to those who appeal to His goodness, believing He is here precisely so that we may entreat Him for divine assistance with our personal needs.

4. Grace for Others

This Presence is finally the treasury of Christ's love, in which He is ready to do wonders for others provided we come to Him with confidence that He will hear our altruistic prayers.

GRACE OF REALIZATION

First of all, our Lord in the Blessed Sacrament is the source of grace we have received to come to Him in the first place. This prior grace underlies all the others. We know we cannot do anything supernatural without Christ. Thus, we certainly would not be inclined to adore Him in the Holy Eucharist unless He had already given us the light and the desire to do so.

The same holds true of the inclination to express our love for Him and to be drawn to approach Him for whatever we need. Unless Christ had first given us the grace to even open the door of a church or chapel and then come in, tell Him we love Him, trust Him and ask for what we need—unless Christ had first given us this grace of "supernatural instinct"—none of us would be reading this book. Whether you call it the grace of attraction, the grace of appeal or the grace of supernatural impulse, Christ's Real Presence in the Eucharist is a magnet which draws souls to itself so they might want to be present where He is present—to be with Him, near Him and even open our minds in conversation with Him.

During His stay in Palestine, Christ's visible presence was just that. Thousands of people flocked to see Him and hear Him. They just wanted to be in His company and enjoy the comfort of being with Him. Love always wants to be near the one whom it loves. This is dramatically illustrated in the Gospel narrative of Zacchaeus (which is read in Masses for Church dedications). St. Luke tells the story:

He was passing through Jericho and behold there was a man named Zacchaeus. He was a leading publican and he was rich.

And he was trying to see Jesus, who He was, but could not on account of the crowd, because he was of small stature. So he ran ahead and climbed up into a sycamore tree to see Him, for He was going to pass that way.

When Jesus came to the place, He looked up and saw him and said to him, "Zacchaeus, make haste and come down, for I must stay in your house today." So he made haste and came down and welcomed Him joyfully. Upon seeing it, everyone began to complain, saying, "He has gone to be a guest of a man who is a sinner." But Zacchaeus stood and said to the Lord, "Behold, Lord, I give one half of my possessions to the poor, and if I have defaulted anyone of anything, I will restore it fourfold."

Jesus said to him, "Today salvation has come to this house, since he too is a son of Abraham. For the Son of Man came to seek and to save the lost" (Luke 19:1–10).

No wonder this Gospel is read for the dedication of a Catholic church. Christ is present there in the fullness of His Incarnate Divinity. As Christ said to Zacchaeus, "Today salvation has come to this house." In other words, we believe a Catholic church or chapel is a sacred place, a holy place. What makes it holy? The all holy God in human form who is present in the Blessed Sacrament is reserved in those edifices!

Christ was physically and geographically present in Palestine. It was this divine presence which drew Zacchaeus to go out of his way to seek Him. Today the presence of Christ in the Blessed Sacrament is just as magnetic. The same presence of the same Jesus draws human hearts to their Savior. The silent voice from the tabernacle invites us to be near. As He once said, "Come to me all who labor and are heavily burdened and I will refresh you." This is the grace of realization. Christ's presence in the Holy Eucharist, on the foundational level, is a grace of realizing who it is who has chosen to dwell amongst us and then responding accordingly.

EMANATING GRACES

If there is one feature of Christ's visible presence in Palestine, it is the fact that this presence was, in our language, a source of emanating grace. After all, once we believe God took on human flesh—once we believe the God–man breathed our air, ate our food, drank our water, walked on our earth and could be seen with bodily eyes, heard with bodily ears, and touched with bodily hands—once we believe that, is there any limit to what we would expect His very presence to do?

After all, God is the almighty Creator of the universe. He brought the mountains and seas into being out of nothing. When this omnipotence is present, and where it is present, we can expect anything from Him, just because of His presence. We can call this "emanation of grace" or "radiation of grace." Whatever name we call it, this presence of the Almighty in human flesh is bound to be, shall we say, "very productive." His powerful presence can be found today in the Eucharist.

Again, we go back to the Gospels to illustrate what this emanation of grace from Christ means. The episode occurred while Jesus was on His way to the house of Jairus, whose daughter was dying. In fact, by the time Jesus reached Jairus' home, his daughter had already died.

St. Luke describes what happened while Christ was en route to Jairus' home:

> It happened as He (Jesus) went that He was pressed by the crowds and a certain woman for over twelve years had had a hemorrhage and had spent all her means on physicians but could not be cured by anyone, came up behind Him and touched the tassel of His cloak and at once, her hemorrhage

ceased and Jesus said, "Who touched Me?" But as everyone was denying it, even those who were with Him said, "Master, the crowds throng and press upon You, and are You saying who touched Me?"

But Jesus said, "Someone touched Me because I know that power had gone forth from Me."

But the woman, seeing that she had not escaped notice, came up trembling and falling down at His feet, declared in the presence of all the people why she had touched Him, and how she had been healed instantly. And He said to her, "Daughter, your faith has saved you; go in peace" (Luke 8:43–50).

Every detail of this miraculous healing of the woman deserves careful scrutiny. Why? Because it is a perfect example of how Christ's presence on earth radiates grace on people just because He *is* on earth.

The woman had been under doctors' treatment for years, but no one ever helped her. She believed Christ could heal her, but the crowd around Christ was too big. Moreover, she might have been afraid even to talk to Him, not knowing what He would say. So what did she do? She tugged on the hem of Christ's cloak and was instantly cured.

But that is not all. Christ asked, "Who touched Me?" And Peter, always taking the lead for the disciples, said, " 'Who touched Me?' Everybody is pushing and shoving and you ask, 'Who touched Me?' " Christ was not satisfied. He said, "Someone has touched Me." Why? Because "I perceived that power had gone out from Me."

This is the classic text to describe the pouring out of grace from Christ just because He is present—nothing else is necessary. Just because He is really, physically and geographically present on earth.

When we talk about this "emanating grace," we can think of Christ's "emanating power." Omnipotence is radiating divine power—the power to work miracles *through* the humanity God assumed when He took flesh of His Virgin Mother. God became man in order that His omnipotence might be communicated just because He, the living God in human flesh, is in our midst.

This is the divinely revealed truth we believe is being continually verified on earth today. The same omnipotent God become man *is* on earth, and power is going forth from Him. He wants to work miracles through His Real Presence. There is only one condition. If we are to benefit from this Incarnate Omnipotence, we must believe. Recall the lesson taught in the Gospels about the importance of belief. During His public ministry, Jesus worked many miracles. He even raised the dead back to life. But His almighty power could be incredibly prevented from being exercised when and where it met the unwillingness to believe. During Christ's visible stay on earth, lack of faith always became a barrier to His emanating power. Christ did work miracles, but on the condition that someone was willing to believe—to believe God had become man and this man who is God is on earth.

So it is today. The living Christ is on earth in the Holy Eucharist no less truly and really than He was at the dawn of Christianity. He not only can, but He wants to work signs and wonders in this world He created. He does work miracles, constantly, now through the humanity which He possesses as God. But we have to believe.

P R A Y E R

LORD JESUS, YOU ARE REALLY PRESENT IN THE BLESSED SACRAMENT. WE THANK YOU FOR THIS GRACE OF REALIZING THAT YOU ARE HERE WITH US AND AMONG US, NO LESS THAN YOU WERE AMONG YOUR DISCIPLES IN THE FIRST CENTURIES OF CHRISTIANITY. WE ALSO THANK YOU FOR ENABLING US THAT YOU ARE HERE AS THE FOUNTAIN OF GRACES THAT WE NEED TO REACH OUR HEAVENLY DESTINY. WE BEG YOU TO ENABLE US TO SEE HOW DEEPLY OUR LIVES DEPEND ON YOURS. WITHOUT YOU WE COULD DO NOTHING ON OUR WAY TO THAT CELESTIAL GOAL FOR WHICH WE WERE MADE. AMEN.

10

TREASURY OF GOD'S BLESSING FOR OURSELVES AND OTHERS

So far, we have seen how the Real Presence of Christ in the Eucharist gives us what we call "the grace of realization." Our Lord enlightens our minds and inspires our wills with the foundational grace of realizing His physical presence on earth and responding to this faith by coming to Him in the Holy Eucharist. We have also seen how Christ's Presence in the Blessed Sacrament is the fountain of graces, emanating from Him out to the whole world, radiating divine power and even working miracles for those who believe.

Now, we go on to explain how Christ in the Blessed Sacrament is a source of actual graces by granting the needs of those who appeal to His goodness. Then after seeing how the Blessed Sacrament provides for all we truly need, we will examine how the Real Presence is a treasury of God's love, in which He is ready to do wonders for others, provided we come to Him with trustful confidence.

SOURCE OF ACTUAL GRACES FOR OURSELVES

In order to appreciate the Real Presence as our source of actual graces, we should briefly explain what the Church means by "actual graces." An actual grace is a temporary supernatural intervention by God to enlighten the mind or strengthen the will to perform supernatural actions that lead to heaven. Actual grace is divine assistance which enables us to obtain, retain or grow in supernatural grace and the life of God. For the sake of completeness, we should add that in God's providence, He uses persons, places and things as instruments or channels of actual graces which enlighten and inspire us on our road to heaven. In God's providential plan, He wants everything in our lives to be a channel of grace.

One of the most authoritative documents explaining how to understand the Real Presence as a source of actual graces is the Encyclical *Mediator Dei* of Pope Pius XII. In this document, he traces to the Church's earliest days the practice of adoring Christ in the Blessed Sacrament. Unfortunately for Catholics today, books and journals dripping with error are telling them adoration of our Lord in the Holy Eucharist is a dispensable exercise. Many Catholics are being told the only reason the Blessed Sacrament is reserved in the tabernacle is to provide Holy Communion for those who are sick or unable to receive by coming personally to Church.

But the faith of the early Christians tells us of the rich history of Eucharistic adoration. In the first three hundred years of the Church's history, there could not even be any churches. "Churches" were all underground. The Blessed Sacrament was reserved to provide for those especially awaiting trial and possible execution for their Catholic faith. But this Jesus was always adored even after Mass and outside of Mass and tended to be the object of special veneration. Once we believe Jesus is really on earth in the Eucharist, we can easily understand how the Church, under the inspiration of the Holy Spirit, has uncovered the depths of what this means and the corresponding practices of piety.

Pope Pius XII also points out how the worship of our Lord in the Eucharist and begging for His grace is a witness to the development of doctrine in the Catholic Church. The following quotation is lengthy but its teaching is basic to our understanding of the Real Presence:

[The Eucharist] contains, as we all know, "truly, really and substantially" the Body and Blood, together with the Soul and Divinity of our Lord Jesus Christ.

Therefore, it is no wonder that the Church, since her origin, has adored the Body of Christ under the species of bread. St. Augustine affirms, "But no one eats the Flesh, unless he has first adored it," adding that "not only do we not sin by adoring, but that we do sin in not adoring."

From these principles of doctrine was born and has developed, step by step, the worship of adoration of the Eucharist distinct from the Holy Sacrifice. This worship of adoration rests upon a valid and solid motive. For the Eucharist is both a Sacrifice and a sacrament. It differs from the other sacraments because it not only produces grace, but it contains in a permanent way the very Author of grace.

The Church commands us to adore Christ hidden under the Eucharistic veils and ask Him for the supernatural and earthly gifts which we always need (*Mediator Dei,* 129–131).

Notice what we are being told. We are told the Church *commands* us to adore Christ in the Blessed Sacrament and to ask Him for the gifts we always need. Another name for those gifts that come from God is actual grace. We are in constant need of actual graces for a number of reasons: to know God's will at every moment of the day, to know how God wants us to do His will every day, to be ready to do God's will once we know what He wants and to actually do God's will in every action we consciously perform.

Go through the Gospels and what do we find? We find person after person asking Jesus for whatever they needed, or actually, for whatever they wanted. Christ would respond favorably if He knew the person really needed what he or she was asking for. This faith in Christ's Real Presence on earth inspired them to adore Him, and they adored Him by begging Him to grant their requests but always implicitly, to grant what they *need*.

So today, that is why Jesus Christ is on earth in the Holy Eucharist— that we may come to Him to tell Him that we love Him, to adore Him as our Incarnate God, to plead with Him to be merciful to us sinners, to pray that He grant us not what *we* want, but what *He* wants. In other words, to meet our needs. This is so important. One of the most necessary actual graces for which we should beg our Lord in the Eucharist is to enlighten our minds to distinguish between what we want and what we need. That is why I like the translation of the Beatitudes that says: "Happy are those who hunger and thirst for what is right" (Matthew 5:6).

TREASURY OF GOD'S BLESSINGS TO OTHERS

Finally, the Holy Eucharist as the Real Presence is meant to be a treasury of God's blessings to others; but we need to discover this treasury at our disposal if we are to obtain for others the immeasurable graces found in the Blessed Sacrament.

First, the power of the Real Presence to provide us with the graces we need personally does not stop with just ourselves. Christ now on earth in the Holy Eucharist wants us also to come to Him and entreat Him to bless others with His grace. As we read the Gospels, we may be astonished at how often people approached Jesus to ask Him to bless others. One of the most memorable events of this altruistic charity, (as opposed to selfish charity in which we love others only as long as and insofar as they love us) was the occasion of a Roman centurion. He came to Jesus asking Him to cure the centurion's servant who was at the point of death. Christ obliged and was on His way to the centurion's house when the centurion sent messages to Jesus to stop Him.

They relayed the centurion's request: "Lord, do not trouble yourself, for I am not worthy that You should come under my roof. But only say the word, and my servant will be healed" (Matthew 8:8). It is not coincidental that the Church has chosen these words of the Roman centurion to say at Mass before we receive our Lord in Holy Communion.

On the last day, we shall be judged mainly on our practice of altruistic charity—our selfless love for others—by meeting their needs.

So we ask ourselves: What is the highest form of charity that we can practice toward others?

The answer: The highest form of charity we can practice toward others is to meet their needs. Meeting people's wants is not charity. Authentic, altruistic charity is meeting people's needs.

We ask again: What is the greatest need others have?

We answer: The greatest need others have is the grace of God.

One more question: Where can we most effectively obtain these graces that others so constantly need?

Answer: At the foot of the tabernacle or before the exposed monstrance, where Jesus Christ is really present in the fullness of His incarnate divine love—a treasury of graces for others.

P R A Y E R

DEAR LORD, WE BELIEVE YOU ARE ON EARTH FOR A REASON. THAT REASON IS THAT WE MIGHT COME TO YOU, ADORE YOU, OUR GOD, AND BEG YOU FOR WHAT WE PERSONALLY NEED AND TO ENTREAT YOU TO GRANT OTHERS WHAT THEY MOST NEED, WHICH IS YOUR GRACE. OPEN THE EYES OF OUR MINDS TO SEE THE MEANING OF WHAT WE BELIEVE SO THAT BELIEVING AND UNDERSTANDING, WE MAY PRACTICE OUR FAITH BY COMING TO YOU AND BEING INFALLIBLY SURE THAT YOU WILL OBTAIN FOR US AND FOR OTHERS WHAT WE AND THEY NEED ON ONE CONDITION: THAT WE BELIEVE THAT YOU ARE OUR GOD WHO BECAME MAN TO GIVE US WHAT WE NEED. AMEN.

11

WHY DID CHRIST INSTITUTE THE HOLY EUCHARIST AS HIS BODILY PRESENCE ON EARTH?

In earlier chapters, we have examined what we believe when we say we believe in the Real Presence. Our focus in the first phase of this book was on understanding the essential elements of our Catholic faith in the Holy Eucharist. We concluded with explaining the meaning of the Eucharist as Sacrifice Sacrament, Communion Sacrament and Presence Sacrament.

In this second phase of this book, we will concentrate on the reason *why* Christ instituted the Holy Eucharist as His bodily presence on earth. God became man when Jesus was conceived and born of His Virgin Mother. He suffered and died on the Cross. Then He rose from the dead and ascended into heaven. Close the first chapter of the book of Christianity. We are now asking ourselves not why God became man, but why the God–man remains on earth in the Eucharist.

Why did Christ do this? In one sense, we have already seen, implicitly, why Jesus did what He did. He wanted to provide us with what the Church has come to call the triple form of the Holy Eucharist as Mass, Holy Communion and the Real Presence. But our purpose here is to probe deeper, and to make more explicit what we have seen so far. Our aim now is to more clearly answer the question, Why?

The comprehensive answer is that Christ gave us the Eucharist so He might give us His grace through the Mass, Holy Communion and the Real Presence. However, this book will now concentrate on the third of these motives, the Real Presence. Christ gave us the Eucharist through transubstantiation in order to provide us with His real, physical, bodily, corporeal, geographical, local presence in the Blessed Sacrament. In other words, He instituted the Holy Eucharist to be present on earth outside the Sacrifice of the Mass besides giving us Holy Communion.

The words "outside" and "besides" are being so widely challenged at the present time, especially since the Second Vatican Council. Some people are actually afraid to use the words "Real Presence." Or as one prominent writer said in an article for a national journal, "Eucharistic Adoration is an outmoded superstition."

We had better be sure our minds know what we do when we come before our Lord in the Holy Eucharist and pour out our hearts to Him in the Blessed Sacrament. Are we practicing "an outmoded superstition"?

WHY THE REAL PRESENCE?

Given the magnitude of the subject, I can only give an overview of this mystery in this book. There are four levels to the answer to our basic question, Why did Jesus institute the Holy Eucharist as the Real Presence? He did so:

- For the *manifestation* of His wisdom and power, His love and infinite mercy.
- For the *communication* of His grace to us and to others through us.
- For the *profession* of our faith, hope and charity.
- For our *imitation* of His humility, poverty, charity, patience and obedience.

The purpose of this book is to enlighten the mind in order to inspire the will. The mystery of the Real Presence is to be lived. In the later chapters, we will go into more detail examining each of these four fundamental motives for Christ giving us His Bodily Presence on earth.

All the reasons for the Real Presence can be summarized in four words: manifestation, communication, profession and imitation. As we look more closely at these reasons, we see the first two (manifestation and communication) pertain to Jesus Christ. The second two (profession and imitation) pertain to us. In other words, Christ is on earth in the fullness of His Incarnate Deity not only to give us something, but also to receive something from us.

MANIFESTATION AND COMMUNICATION

Manifestation: On His side, Christ remains on earth to reveal Himself as God made man in the basic attributes of His divinity, namely, His wisdom, power, love and mercy. He instituted the Real Presence in order to manifest these divine perfections.

Communication: Also on His side, Christ is on earth in the Eucharist to continue His Incarnation by giving us what we most need—the graces He merited on Calvary. These graces are both personal and apostolic. On the personal level, Christ communicates His grace to us for our salvation and sanctification. He enlightens our minds and strengthens our wills through His grace in the Real Presence.

But Christ also gives us grace to be apostles of His grace to others. We may define the apostolate as "the channeling of grace." The apostolate is to channel grace from Christ, through us, to others. We are effective as communicators of Christ's grace to others only as we are possessed of His grace ourselves. We can best obtain these graces for others from the Real Presence of Christ in the Holy Eucharist.

PROFESSION AND IMITATION

Christ also gave us His Real Presence because He expects a response from us. That response is on two levels, profession and imitation.

Profession: Through the Real Presence, Christ wants us to profess our faith and hope in Him and our selfless love for Him.

We may profess our faith in Him as God who became man to be our saving Lord. There is nothing in Christianity which requires a more profound profession of faith than the Real Presence. Believing in the Real Presence means believing in everything which God has revealed. Faith in the Real Presence comprehends faith in the whole of divine revelation.

We may also profess our hope in Him as our final destiny, and on earth, as a source of all the help we need to enlighten our dark minds and strengthen our pathetically weak wills.

Through His Real Presence, we also profess our love for Him who loves us so much, thus enabling and motivating our love for others. If the Real Presence is the highest profession of God's love for us, why did He institute the Holy Eucharist as the Real Presence? To show us how much He loves us. Christ had no merely academic purpose. His purpose was to evoke our love in return.

Imitation: Christ also expects us to respond to His Real Presence by imitating Him in His Eucharistic life now on earth. He wants us to pattern our lives not only on the Jesus described in the Gospels whom we meet in history, but on Jesus in His present Eucharistic Reality, whom we meet today.

PRAYER

EUCHARISTIC JESUS, WE THANK YOU FOR INSTITUTING YOUR REAL PRESENCE ON EARTH. THANKS TO THIS GREAT GIFT WE CAN SPEAK TO YOU NOW JUST AS TRULY AS THE APOSTLES SPOKE TO YOU IN PALESTINE. YOU CAN HEAR US NOW NO LESS THAN YOU HEARD THOSE WHO CAME TO YOU DURING YOUR PHYSICAL PRESENCE ON EARTH. WE KNOW YOU ARE OUR GOD WHOSE LOVE INSPIRED YOU TO GIVE US YOURSELF TO COME TO YOU, PRESENT AMONG US BUT VISIBLE TO OUR EYES OF FAITH. WE KNOW YOU WILL HEAR US AS SURELY AS YOU HEARD YOUR DISCIPLES TWO THOUSAND YEARS AGO. WHY? BECAUSE WE BELIEVE. AMEN.

12

THE REAL PRESENCE: MANIFESTATION OF CHRIST'S ATTRIBUTES OF WISDOM, POWER, LOVE AND MERCY

We now begin our reflections on why Christ instituted the Eucharist as His bodily presence on earth. In this chapter, we will see that Christ did so in order to manifest His divine attributes of wisdom, power, love and mercy.

Of course we know that even before the Incarnation, God had manifested Himself through the world He created. The human mind could come to some knowledge of the existence and attributes of God by reasoning on the marvels of His creation. But not all people recognize God in His wonderful creations. St. Paul tells us the pagan world of his day, specifically the Roman world, was so ungodly in its conduct because it was so godless in its mind. They did not merely fail to believe, but refused to recognize the possibility of believing in God from the work of His hands. Paul says these people are blameworthy for not seeing God. "Since the creation of the world, His invisible attributes of everlasting power and His divinity have been understood through things that He made. And so they have no excuse" (Romans 1:20).

What more could God do to reveal Himself? In His infinite goodness, God became man by His Incarnation. This is the cardinal truth of Christianity on which everything else depends and from which everything else derives. As we have been saying, the Holy Eucharist—the Real Presence—gathers all of its meaning from the fact of the Incarnation.

But why did God become man? For two basic reasons. First, God became man so that He might assume a human free will and by His death on the Cross, freely sacrifice His human life for our salvation. It is both that simple and that profound. God became man so that He might have a body and a soul that could separate at death. He became man not only that He might be able to die, but that He might die willingly, using His free will and thus voluntarily sacrificing His human life for the salvation of a sinful human race.

Secondly, having become man, God wanted to not only be man long enough to die on the Cross and redeem the world, He became Incarnate so He might remain Incarnate for all eternity. The first reason for the Incarnation was satisfied, in time, on Calvary. The second reason will go on forever. Not only did God want to die for us; He wanted to live as one of us—the God–man as the object of our veneration and the continuing cause of our salvation.

THE INCARNATION NOW ON EARTH

Before we take up each one of the four attributes of God, we should say something about the Real Presence as the Incarnation now on earth. Faith tells us that Christ, who is God Incarnate, was crucified, died, was buried, rose from the dead and ascended into Heaven. But our Catholic faith tells us much more. It tells us that the same Incarnate God, who is at the right hand of His Heavenly Father, is also on earth in the Holy Eucharist. To know this is to know the meaning of the Holy Eucharist. Not to know this is not to really understand what the Eucharist means.

Pope Pius XII beautifully expressed the meaning of the Eucharist a year before he became Pope. As Eugenio Cardinal Pacelli, he went to Hungary to represent his predecessor, Pius XI, at the International Eucharistic Congress in Budapest in 1938, just a year before the outbreak of the Second World War. The theme of Cardinal Pacelli's address at the Congress was that Christ had indeed left this earth in visible form at His Ascension. But He is emphatically still on earth—the Jesus of history, continuing to dwell among us in the Sacrament of the altar. That is the Real Presence. On these premises, we must say Christ is in the Holy Eucharist as the Incarnate second person of the Trinity. Therefore, in the Real Presence, He is the Incarnate manifestation of His divine attributes of wisdom, power, love and mercy. We are now ready to take up each one of these four attributes.

WISDOM

The Real Presence is the manifestation of the wisdom of God. The theme of St. John's Gospel is that the Word of God, which is the wisdom of God, became flesh and dwelt among us. St. Paul told the Corinthians, "Christ [is] the wisdom of God" (1 Corinthians 1:24). Paul urged the Colossians to know "the mystery of God, the Father of Jesus, in whom are all the treasures of wisdom and knowledge" (Colossians 2:3). Since Christ is the Incarnate wisdom of God, then the Incarnate wisdom not only dwelt (past tense) but *dwells* (present tense) among us. When St. John tells us the God-made man "dwelt" among us, the inspired Greek word for "dwelt" means to dwell geographically, spatially, being with or among those with whom someone dwells. If St. John said Christ dwelt among us during His visible stay in Palestine, we must say the same about Christ dwelling among us today in the Real Presence. Christ is not only "dwelling" among us in heaven but here on earth in the Holy Eucharist.

This dwelling is crucial. In other words, because of the institution of the Blessed Sacrament, Christ, the Incarnate wisdom of God, is present to us as we are present to Him. For example, you would have no doubt if you were to say to yourself, "I am here." That is a safe statement. Well, in the same profound sense, Christ is here in the Eucharist. The all-wise God who became man is on earth so that He might be the object of our constant adoration.

As we enter into this phase of the book, let us remember that these facts about the Eucharist are more than abstract truths. These truths are to be put into practice. Christ is here in the Holy Eucharist to receive from us the humble submission of our proud minds to His infinite wisdom. There is only one condition: that we acknowledge His presence in our midst as the Incarnate Son of God. Adoration before the Blessed Sacrament means many things, but its primary meaning is the veneration of what looks like bread but which we recognize as the infinite wisdom of God Himself who became man and now lives in our midst as the all-wise ruler of the universe. That is a lot of adoration!

In the Eucharist, we adore Him with our minds and our wills because we cannot dissociate our body from our souls. Not yet. As we sadly know, we can come before the Blessed Sacrament in body, but the mind can be anywhere. But to adore our Lord in the Blessed Sacrament, we should submit both our minds and our wills to the almighty wisdom of God made manifest to us today in Christ's Real Presence in the Holy Eucharist.

POWER

Christ also instituted the Holy Eucharist in order to manifest His divine attribute of power. Running as a theme throughout the New Testament is the fact that Christ was indeed the all-powerful God who became a helpless child to redeem us. In the closing verses of Matthew's Gospel, Christ made it clear that "all power is given to me in Heaven and on earth" (Matthew 28:18). The miracles Christ performed were all manifestations of His divine power. Jesus spoke with human lips and touched with human hands, but the power behind those words and hands was the almighty power of God. That is why Christ worked miracles. By His divine power, He calmed the storm at sea with a single word. He healed the blind, the deaf and the dumb. He cured paralytics by a touch of His human hand. He walked on the waters and gave Peter the power to do the same for as long as the apostle trusted in that power. Christ called the dead Lazarus from the grave. As the crowning proof of His divine power, He raised Himself from the grave.

That same Almighty Jesus is present in the Holy Eucharist. The Real Presence is Incarnate Omnipotence. If there is one act of faith we should make as we adore Christ in the Blessed Sacrament, it should be the absolute, unswerving confidence in His divine power. One reason He allows us to make fools of ourselves and fall flat on our faces is that we might pick ourselves up and go to Him and tell Him, "Dear Lord, thanks for humiliating me. But you, being my God, have the power to do what you want with me. Bend my will to your will." We can always turn to His divine power manifested in His Real Presence in the Holy Eucharist.

LOVE

We now reflect on why God became man and instituted the Eucharist as a manifestation of His divine love. First, we turn to St. John's unforgettable definition of God: "God is love" (1 John 4:8). Again in his Gospel, John tells us "God so loved the world that He gave His only begotten Son that those who believe in Him may not perish but may have life everlasting" (John 3:16). God, who is love, became man so that *Love* may live among us—not only as a grateful memory, but as a present reality. This is the meaning of the Real Presence.

We return to the Eucharist as the manifestation of divine love. We ask, "Could God in His infinite wisdom have been more inventive?" To love someone means to become as much as possible like the one who is loved. God became man, like human beings in all things but sin. This God who became man is here on earth today in the Blessed Sacrament. To love someone means to want to be near the one who is loved.

Proximity of place is a sign of intimacy of love. Could God who became man be closer to us in space than He is in the Eucharist?

Moreover, to be present is much more than being near or close to someone. To be present means to think of the one and to love the one to whom you are present. God became man so that as man with human thoughts He might be thinking of us here on earth. He became man with a human will so He might be loving us here on earth. The obvious implication is to evoke our corresponding response in return. It is not pious fancy but a mystery of faith that God chose to take on human flesh and blood and take a human mind and human will in order to be with us, near us, close to us, geographically, in the Holy Eucharist as a manifestation of His love for us.

MERCY

Over the centuries, the Church has been teaching that of all the divine attributes, the mercy of God is the crown. It is the highest, the deepest and for us, the most important divine attribute. Let us remind ourselves what mercy is. Mercy is love indeed, but much more. Mercy is love that forgives. Mercy is love that endures. Mercy is love that suffers. Mercy is love that loves those who do not love. Mercy is love that gives to those who do not deserve to be loved. Mercy is love that is ready to die for those whom it loves.

Given this framework of our faith, it is clear that Christ is the Incarnation of Divine Mercy. Incidentally, this is our present Holy Father's favorite definition of Christ. This is why God became man—in order to be able to practice mercy in His own person by suffering and dying on the Cross out of love for a sin-laden human race. When we say that, we need to make sure we do not think of that sinful human race in abstract terms. Always include oneself. God became man and died for me. The Incarnation of Divine Mercy died for me.

It is this merciful God Incarnate who instituted the Holy Eucharist on the night before He died in order that He might remain with us on earth until the end of time. The conclusion for us is obvious. Yes, we are to adore our Lord really present in the Blessed Sacrament. But this adoration should be very clear. The Christ whom we worship in the Eucharist is the God of mercy, who shed His Blood on the Cross to make the Eucharist possible. The one whom we are adoring is God who became man so He might have human blood in His veins—blood now glorified, but blood that dropped to the ground on Calvary as proof of His merciful love.

Anytime we forget that Christ in the Holy Eucharist is here with His human blood, we fall short of really understanding the Real Presence. The reality present on earth is the wisdom of God. The reality here on earth is the power of God. This reality is the love of God. This reality is the mercy of God, who became flesh and blood and lives among us so that we might live with Him here in this valley of tears by faith and in the blessed eternity of seeing Him in the life to come.

P R A Y E R

My Eucharistic Jesus, You are Incarnate mercy who became man out of love for me. Grant me the grace that I most need in this valley of tears, the grace to love You in a way that corresponds to Your love for me. You became man to be able to die on the Cross to prove Your love for me. Grant me, dear Jesus, the grace to prove my love for You by dying on my Cross out of love for You. Amen.

13

THE REAL PRESENCE AS COMMUNICATION OF GRACE

We have been asking, Why did Christ institute the Eucharist as the Real Presence? In this chapter, we will look at how Christ gave us the Real Presence as a communication of His grace.

The most powerful source of Christ's grace comes from adoring our Lord in the Blessed Sacrament. Our purpose here is to focus on Eucharistic adoration as this potent fountain of graces. We will discuss how petition is an important part of Eucharistic adoration and then explain how devotion to the Holy Eucharist is "bilateral." We are indeed called to communicate to our Lord in the Eucharist, but He is also communicating with us. In fact, unless He were first communicating His grace to us, we could not even begin to communicate with Him.

So in this chapter, we look at the Church's understanding of Eucharistic adoration not so much from our side, but, if you will, from Christ's side. To do this, we will answer three questions:

1. How does Eucharistic adoration include Eucharistic petition?
2. Why is Eucharistic petition a powerful means for Christ communicating His grace?
3. What is the apostolate of Eucharistic prayer?

PETITIONS AS PART OF EUCHARISTIC ADORATION

First, we are not trifling with words when we say adoration of the Eucharist includes petition. Why is it important to know this? Because otherwise, we are liable to deprive ourselves and others of many blessings Christ intends to give us and others through our fervent petitions before Him in the Blessed Sacrament. In technical language, adoration is the act of religion by which God is recognized as alone worthy of supreme honor because He is infinitely perfect and has a right to our total obedience as our Creator and total dedication as our destiny.

Thus we find adoration includes every form of prayer, including the petitions by which we ask God for what we need and for what others need. What are we doing when we ask God for something? We are acknowledging our complete dependence on Him for everything that we have received in the past, that we have now and that we hope for in the future. You can see how we adore our Lord when we humbly acknowledge our utter dependence on Him in our petitions.

Now we can ask how adoration in general differs from Eucharist adoration. Is there any difference? Does it make a difference?

Yes. There is a crucial difference. After all, adoring God in general is not the same as believing the three fundamental truths underlying Eucharistic adoration. Yes, every time we ask God for something we are adoring Him. But it is one thing to adore God in general, and it is something quite distinct to first believe that God became man, that Jesus Christ *is* God become man and that Jesus Christ, the God–man, is really present in the Holy Eucharist, and then adore Him.

Five times a day almost one billion Muslims throughout the world bow in profound adoration to Allah, turning always in the direction of Mecca. Are they adoring God? Yes, because Allah for them is the one infinite creator of heaven and earth. But no Muslim in his right mind would ever bow or prostrate himself before the Blessed Sacrament. So profound is the difference between general adoration of God (no matter how authentic) and Eucharistic adoration that since the middle of the twentieth century, two million Catholics in the Sudan have been starved to death by the Muslims for adoring Jesus Christ as though he were Allah. But *Isa*, which is the Arabic for Jesus, is God.

Here in fact is the basic difference between all Christian and non-Christian religions: Non-Christians may believe in God, but they vehemently, virulently deny that God became man and became the Son of Mary in the person of Jesus Christ. Moreover, here lies the basic difference between Catholic Christianity and the form of Christianity that separated from the Church in the sixteenth century. As Catholics, we believe Jesus Christ is physically on earth in the Holy Eucharist. The inheritors of the so-called reformation do not believe this. In fact, this difference is so deep that several of my fellow Jesuits who came before me died as martyrs for their steadfast devotion to the Holy Eucharist. They were persecuted because the inheritors of the reformation considered these devout Catholics "idolators" for adoring our Lord in the Eucharist.

In summary, we ask, when we adore Christ in the Blessed Sacrament, should we beg Him for His grace? Emphatically, yes! When we ask Him for light and strength for ourselves and for others, are we adoring Christ in the Holy Eucharist? Again, emphatically, yes! This prayer of adoring petition presumes faith in Christ's divinity, and with resounding emphasis, presumes faith in the Real Presence. Thus, our Eucharistic petitions are an important part of Eucharistic adoration.

EUCHARISTIC PETITIONS AS A SOURCE OF GRACE

Now we need to examine how our Eucharistic petitions are a powerful source of God's grace. In order for Christ to communicate His grace, He wants us to communicate with Him through petitions. If we reflect on those Gospel scenes when people petitioned Christ, two things stand out with luminous clarity:

1. The contemporaries of Christ asked Him for many things. Most of His miracles, we may believe, were the answers to these petitions.
2. Christ repeatedly told His followers (not just His contemporaries, but His followers for all times) to ask for what they needed, and He assured us that whatever we ask for in His name He will always grant. As we reread the Gospels, there is a close relationship between asking Christ and receiving from Christ. Ask and you shall receive. If we do not ask, we shall not receive. Receive what? What Christ would have given us had we asked Him.

There is another striking feature about these Gospel petitioners as described by the evangelists. The people who asked for favors from Christ made sure they were near Christ. Some of them even shoved and pushed and made a nuisance of themselves to get near their Savior. His presence inspired people to come to Him and ask Him to work some miracle which they believed only He could perform. There was a remarkable nearness of place or space between the petitioner and Christ when the Savior responded favorably to what was asked of Him.

That is why prayer before the Blessed Sacrament is such a potent source of blessings which are communicated by Christ to the one who asks Him and is near to Him. The one who is praying believes Christ is truly present in the Blessed Sacrament. The one praying comes physically close to Christ in the Eucharist as an intimate expression of faith in Christ's power to grant requests which we make in our prayers. The one praying believes there is not a more effective way of obtaining favors from God than to ask the God–man Himself present in the sacrament of His love.

THE APOSTOLATE OF EUCHARISTIC PRAYER

Christ does communicate His graces to those who come to Him in prayerful petition for His aid. But what needs to be stressed is that

Eucharistic prayer is a source of grace not only for the one praying, but also for those for whom the Eucharistic adoration–petition is made.

Call it apostolic prayer to our Lord in the Holy Eucharist or call it the Eucharistic Apostolate. By whatever name you give it, these petitions for others before our Lord in the Blessed Sacrament are an essential part of our faith in the Real Presence as communication of grace. I know no one who was more insistent on this than St. Peter Julian Eymard, the founder of the Blessed Sacrament Fathers. He asked, "What should the Eucharistic adorers pray for?" He answered:

> Eucharistic prayer has an additional merit: it goes straight to the Heart of God like a flaming dart; it makes Jesus work, act, and relive in His Sacrament; it releases His power. The adorer does still more; he prays through Jesus Christ and shares our Lord's role as Intercessor with the Father and divine Advocate for His redeemed brethren.
>
> But what should they pray for? The rallying cry, "Thy Kingdom Come" (*Adveniat Regnum Tuum*), expresses for adorers the end and the law of prayer. They should pray that the light of the truth of Jesus Christ may enlighten all men, especially the Infidels, Jews, Heretics and Schismatics, and that they may return to true faith and charity.
>
> They should pray for our Lord's kingdom of holiness in His faithful, His religious, His priests, that He may live in them by love. They should pray above all for the Sovereign Pontiff, for all the intentions dear to his heart; for their own Bishop, for all that his zeal desires to accomplish, for all the priests of the diocese that God may bless their apostolic labors and inflame them with zeal for His glory and with love for Holy Church (*The Real Presence* vol. 1, p. 14).

That is why over the centuries, the Church has been so insistent that contemplative communities be established in mission lands. Why? Because the most powerful source of grace from Christ comes through the silent prayers of pleading adoration offered to our Lord in the Holy Eucharist.

P R A Y E R

LORD, JESUS, WE BELIEVE YOU ARE OUR GOD WHO BECAME MAN. WE BELIEVE YOU ARE THE GOD–MAN WHO INSTITUTED THE HOLY EUCHARIST AS THE PRINCIPAL SOURCE FOR YOUR COMMUNICATING GRACE TO US. BUT DEAR LORD, WE KNOW, AND TEACH US TO KNOW MORE DEEPLY, THAT YOU WILL COMMUNICATE TO US WHAT WE NEED, PROVIDED WE COMMUNICATE OUR NEEDS TO YOU AND THAT WHERE YOU ARE PRESENT IN THE HOLY EUCHARIST, WE TOO ARE PRESENT, SO THAT ASKING YOU FOR WHAT WE NEED, YOU WILL ANSWER OUR PETITIONS BECAUSE YOU ARE OUR GOD. AMEN.

14

THE REAL PRESENCE: PROFESSION OF FAITH

In the last three chapters, we have been asking ourselves why Christ instituted the Real Presence of the Holy Eucharist. So far, we have considered how Christ, through the Real Presence, communicates His graces to those who come to Him in the Eucharist and manifests His divine attributes of wisdom, power, love and mercy. These first two reasons can be summarized by the words "communication" and "manifestation."

Our present focus on why Christ instituted the Real Presence also can be summed up in one word: "profession." Christ gave us the Real Presence in order that we might profess to Him in the Blessed Sacrament our faith, hope and love:

- Our faith in Him as our Lord, Savior and God who became man.
- Our hope in Him as our final destiny.
- Our love for Him and our proof of this love for Him by loving those whom God places into our lives.

We will examine our profession of faith, hope and love in three separate chapters, beginning with profession of faith. In each chapter, we will answer five questions:

1. How do we define these virtues?
2. When must we profess these virtues?
3. When should we profess these virtues?
4. How do we profess these virtues in the Real Presence?
5. What are the benefits of professing these virtues in the Real Presence?

WHAT IS DIVINE FAITH?

Faith in general is the acceptance of something as true on the word of someone else. Thus, every rational human being believes. As children, unless we believed our parents we would not know how to talk or what to say. We believe when we read, when we buy something and when we listen. People believe when they marry. When we go to a restaurant, we believe the food we are eating is not toxic. To believe in what other people tell us is called human faith.

But when the one we believe is God, it is called divine faith. Divine faith is the assent of the intellect to everything God has revealed, not because we can comprehend why, but only because God, who is all-wise and all-truthful, has made the revelation. Unlike human faith, divine faith is impossible without the grace of God. Without grace, we cannot even want to believe. Without continual grace, we cannot continue believing. That is why prayer is so important for faith. Prayer is the principal source of grace. Those who stop praying eventually start to lose their faith. We need grace first for the will, and we need grace for the mind. First, we need grace for the human will to *want* to believe. Then we need grace for the mind to actually assent to God's revealed truth.

WHEN *MUST* WE PROFESS OUR FAITH?

We should first remind ourselves that professing our Catholic faith is not an option. It is our obligation and is necessary for salvation. So we ask, *when* must we profess our faith? Whenever our non-profession would reasonably be interpreted as non-belief. Remember that not professing the faith can be equivalent to denying the faith. Silence can mean consent. Silence can also mean denial.

Not that profession means someone else is somehow either presently or in the future a witness to our profession. Our profession of faith can be verbal with spoken words, or written in a letter or note, or printed.

This profession can also be an artifact, painting or sculpture. Profession of faith can be bodily; we profess our faith with our lips, faces and gestures without saying a word. We profess our faith in song and music and melody. Even music without words professes our faith—either the sound is a profession of the true faith or an opposition to it.

We must profess our faith in order to preserve the faith. Unless someone had professed their faith to us, none of us would be here. All faith is communicated from one believer to another by the believer somehow professing the faith.

WHEN *SHOULD* WE PROFESS OUR FAITH?

We have a duty to profess our faith whenever non-profession would reasonably be interpreted as non-belief, but we should also profess our faith as a means of growing in Christian perfection. The first law of sanctity is to go beyond our obligation of professing the faith. We should profess our faith whenever we know such profession will help us preserve our faith, grow in faith and also help others to receive or grow in faith.

We should remember that God's will is manifest not only through His laws. He also invites us to do His will in ways that are not under the penalty of sin. Thus, when a person becomes a religious, that person decides to profess the faith beyond what is strictly binding under sin. That is the main reason why Christ instituted the consecrated life: so that some people might profess their faith beyond what they would have to do to be saved. When taking vows, a religious obliges himself to profess the faith beyond the precepts of obligation. Incidentally, that is why religious wear a religious habit—as a profession of their faith.

HOW *DO* WE PROFESS OUR FAITH IN
THE REAL PRESENCE?

The way a person professes his faith in the Real Presence will depend on his state of life or circumstances in which he lives. Thus, bishops profess their faith in the Real Presence by seeing that the people of their dioceses pay due respect to the Blessed Sacrament. For example, bishops should ensure that architecture and furnishing of Church buildings and the liturgical practice in parishes reflect and do not hinder the people's faith in Christ's Real Presence in the Holy Eucharist.

Priests also have their distinctive duties and opportunities to profess their faith in the Real Presence. Those consecrated to religious life have their distinct obligations and ways to profess this faith. The faithful should expect their bishops, priests and religious to show their profession of faith in Christ's Real Presence in the Blessed Sacrament.

All the faithful (bishops, priests, religious and laity) *must* profess their faith in the Real Presence by giving due reverence to the Blessed Sacrament. This reverence means genuflecting, kneeling in silence and showing awareness of Christ's Real Presence. This reverence must include some praying before the Blessed Sacrament. During Christ's visible stay on earth, anyone who dimly believed Jesus Christ was who He said He was naturally desired to spend time with Him and showed some awareness of being in His presence. We should have that same desire to spend time with Jesus today in His Real Presence in the Holy Eucharist.

The faithful may profess their faith in the Eucharist by Eucharistic adoration either alone or with others, either in personal devotion or liturgy. Recently, the Holy See established a historically important association called Perpetual Eucharistic Adoration for the laity around the world, for lay people to promote Eucharistic adoration in their parishes and in every diocese in the Catholic Church. These are all ways for us to profess our faith to God in His Real Presence.

BENEFITS

Next we will consider the benefits of professing our faith in the Real Presence; but before we do that, we also need to appreciate how much the Real Presence is being challenged in many nominally Catholic circles today. The following is an excerpt from an article published in a nationally circulating magazine for priests:

> The Christian tradition is filled with duality, heaven–hell, light–darkness, life–death, moral–immoral, body–soul, sacred–profane. The notion that God is absent from certain things, events, acts and people, and therefore, must be "brought in" is a strong foundational belief of fundamentalism. It is certainly not limited to Fundamentalists.
>
> Most often this language of our own "blessings" indicates our belief in this duality. Why do we bless water, bread, wine, another? Most Catholics would answer, "to make them holy" which is to say, to make them not profane.
>
> There was a long tradition of looking at bread and wine as profane things which become holy (the Body and Blood of Jesus) through the words of institution spoken by an ordained priest (the one who brings the sacred into the profane).
>
> However, this is not the primary nor most ancient tradition of the Catholic Church.
>
> The early Church communities gathered for "the breaking of the bread" and "the sharing of the cup." They assembled for *actions*. They knew that the Risen Lord was already present in their midst. It was not a matter of making the Lord present in bread and wine, but using bread and wine to *remember* what Jesus had done for them. But more importantly, to remember what they were called to do—to do what Jesus had done, to *become bread and wine*, to be broken and poured out as nourishment for others.
>
> One person did not make the Lord present. The Risen Lord was present because the community gathered . . . .

The Eucharist is not about duality, sacred versus profane, not about the Risen Lord being present where before he was not. The Eucharist is action and very much about us. The danger with saying "we *receive* the Eucharist" is that we can forget that we are *to be* Eucharist.

The assembly is essential for the Eucharist. All assemblies need a leader. But does the leader of the Eucharistic worship *need to be* an ordained priest, whether male or female, married or not? I think not.

Ordained priests will be part of the assembly in some way, for a long time. But I think the role of the ordained will be seen in a different light once we begin to recapture the sense of what it means for all of us to *be* Eucharist, when we realize we belong to each other.

We cannot emphasize this enough. As never before, we who believe in the Real Presence need to profess our faith in this cardinal mystery of Catholic Christianity. We meet to worship our Lord on earth in the Blessed Sacrament as often as we can, for as long as we can and as fervently as we can. Somebody, somewhere had better profess faith in Christ's Real Presence on earth in the Holy Eucharist because the Catholic Church will be able to exist and survive only where and as long as there are still such believers. Faith is absolutely essential to life. The benefits are manifold. Such profession will deepen our own understanding of what the Real Presence means. There is no more effective way known in the history of the Church for growing and deepening one's faith in the Real Presence than by professing it and "living" it.

Such profession will also clarify in our minds how the presence of Christ in the Eucharist is absolutely unique. We may speak of Christ's presence "everywhere," but His real, bodily, Eucharistic presence is as unique as was His visible presence on earth in first-century Palestine.

Professing our faith in the Real Presence will strengthen our ability to profess it to others. Only convinced people are courageous people. "I have believed. Therefore have I spoken." Those who are not sure and have doubts are not courageous. It takes courage to profess our faith in all the mysteries. Such profession of faith in the Real Presence will enable us to defend the Real Presence, even against hostile forces in our lives. This profession will help convert those who have lost their faith in the Real Presence and help them return to the truth that Jesus Christ is on earth in the Holy Eucharist.

Professing our faith in the Eucharist will also bring graces to those who never knew Jesus Christ and help them discover that He is here. I would like to mention one of my happy memories from over the years concerning a Jewish girl in Manhattan. She came to visit me because she was curious about the Catholic faith. I asked her, "What aroused your curiosity?" She said, "I didn't quite know what I was doing, but I sneaked into the back of the Chapel and in just a few minutes realized what I never realized before. Jesus Christ, the one in whom Christians believe, is here." Her life was changed by the experience, and so was mine in instructing her in the faith.

Once you believe in the Real Presence, you do not have to say a thing. God will use you to channel His grace and gift of faith to others. Such profession makes our lives here on earth a prelude for that eternal life where we will no longer have to believe; because face-to-face we will see Jesus Christ, the Son of God who became the son of Mary, to give us the Real Presence as our greatest possession here on earth and our destiny in the life to come.

P R A Y E R

LORD JESUS, TRULY PRESENT IN THE BLESSED SACRAMENT. ALTHOUGH I CANNOT SEE YOU WITH BODILY EYES, THE EYES OF MY MIND TELL ME THAT YOU ARE REALLY HERE. YOU ARE AS TRULY HERE AS YOU WERE ON EASTER SUNDAY MORNING WHEN YOU ADDRESSED THE CONVERTED HEART AND SAID, "MARY." SHE IMMEDIATELY RECOGNIZED WHOSE VOICE IT WAS AND LAY PROSTRATE AT YOUR FEET TO ADORE YOU AS HER GOD. HERE BEFORE THE BLESSED SACRAMENT I NEITHER SEE YOU NOR HEAR YOU, BUT I KNOW YOU ARE HERE. STRENGTHEN MY FAITH, DEAR JESUS, SO THAT LIKE MARY MAGDALEN I MAY BE SENT BY YOU TO PROCLAIM TO EVERYONE WHOM I MEET THAT I BELIEVE IN YOU, MY LORD AND MY GOD. AMEN.

15

THE REAL PRESENCE: PROFESSION OF HOPE

We continue our reflections on why Christ instituted the Real Presence. In this chapter, we will consider the fact that Christ gave us the Real Presence so we might profess our hope in Him as our final destiny.

WHAT IS DIVINE HOPE?

Just as we saw how every human being has faith, every normal human also has hope. Hope in general is the confident desire of obtaining some future good that is difficult to obtain. Consequently, it is a desire which implies seeking and pursuing some future good that is not yet possessed but wanted. Hope and fear are correlatives. We hope for some future good. We fear a future evil. Hope is confident that what is desired will certainly be attained. Therefore, hope is the opposite of despair. Yet, hope recognizes that the object wanted is not easily obtained and that it requires effort to overcome whatever obstacles stand in the way.

Immediately we should distinguish hope from trust. Strictly speaking, we *trust* people; whereas, we *hope* to obtain what those people have promised. As with faith, there is human hope and divine hope. Human hope is the confident desire of obtaining some future good from human beings, and that is what we live on—trusting certain people. In the measure that we trust them, we hope that we will obtain what they have assured us. That is human hope.

Divine hope is not natural; it is supernatural. It is the confident desire of obtaining from God two things: the heaven which He promised to those who serve Him faithfully and the necessary means to reach this eternal destiny. These are not semantic distinctions. Our faith and hope depend on our understanding what we believe and what we hope for.

Like divine faith, divine hope is impossible without the grace of God. First we need God's grace to trust that He will give us the graces we need to even believe in heaven. Then we need God's grace to be confident He will bring us to heaven, provided we are faithful in doing His will. The greatest danger to our hope in God's promises is the memory of our own infidelity. In other words, we are confident God will give us what He promised, but the measure of our confidence is the degree to which we know we have been faithful. Heaven indeed requires divine grace. It is not enough that God offers the grace to reach heaven. We must also accept, and cooperate with, that grace.

WHEN *MUST* WE PROFESS OUR HOPE?

Note the imperative. We *must* periodically profess our hope throughout life. We must specifically profess our hope whenever we are tempted against the virtue of hope, as when laboring under heavy worry or anxiety or when under stress or discouragement or when we face a duty we must fulfill but are overwhelmed by the dread of our own weakness or expected failure. The more we are troubled and the more severely we are tempted, the more liable we are to discouragement, self-doubt, depression or despair. To make sure we do not give in to discouragement and despair, we must cultivate the habit of professing our hope.

WHEN *SHOULD* WE PROFESS OUR HOPE?

Professing our hope under heavy trial or temptation is a must. But we are also encouraged to profess our hope every day. Masters of the spiritual life tell us to make acts of hope at least as aspirations frequently, regularly and even habitually. Those who should make more frequent and more fervent acts of hope are those whom God calls to a life of consecrated perfection, to the priesthood, to marriage and raising of a Christian family, and those who by nature are more prone to worry or discouragement (what psychologists call the melancholic temperament). Why should we profess our hope regularly? The difficulties and responsibilities people face in today's world are naturally insurmountable. We all should profess our hope in God's promises regularly in order to obtain more grace from God, to help us persevere in being faithful to our state of life and to grow in the virtue of divine hope. The higher the calling of one's vocation, the more demanding the lifetime commitment. The more unexpected seduction and temptations, the more one should cultivate the habit of professing hope. These are not ordinary days. No wonder such strong efforts are being made throughout the Western world to legalize euthanasia—so much of the Western world has become a hopeless world, dreading pain and running away from the Cross. In today's world, we need to profess our hope more than ever before.

PROFESSING OUR HOPE IN THE REAL PRESENCE

We now ask, "How are we to profess our hope in God's promises as revealed in the Real Presence?" As St. Paul tells us, "Faith is the substance of things hoped for." Faith is the foundation of our hope that God's promises will indeed be fulfilled.

Our hope is only as strong as our faith. Our hope is only as confident as our faith is sound. Our hope is only as courageous as our faith in God and His goodness is unshakable. Those who believe in God hope to obtain from Him what He promised. Believing people are hopeful people. Unbelieving people are hopeless people.

What does faith tell us about the Real Presence? It tells us God so loved the world that He became man and died on the Cross to redeem us by His Blood. Faith also tells us that on the night before He died, that same God who became man chose to change bread and wine into His own living Self, the Incarnate God. We believe God became man not only to die on the Cross, but also to be with us, near us, next to us; and when we receive Him in Holy Communion, within us. Not to hope in this God when by faith we know how much He has loved us would be sheer madness!

Faith is the evidence of things unseen—"the substance of things hoped for." We should note that Christ's contemporaries in Palestine had more evidence for their belief than we do. They could see a man who walked, talked, ate, drank and got tired. But they still had to believe that this man was God. Our faith is twice tested; we do not even see a man! We see what looks like bread or tastes like wine, and we believe that behind these appearances is a man and that man is the Incarnate God.

Faith tells us that this same Jesus, who said, "Have confidence, I have overcome the world," is here on earth giving us the same message today, assuring us that He will provide the help we need in this life. Whatever it is, He promises to give us all we need to cope with the trials of this world and the light and strength we need to reach our eternal destiny in heaven.

We must note how crucially important it is for us to distinguish divine hope from human hope. Unlike human hope, divine hope may be painful! Even in symbolic language, anybody in his right mind knows that heaven is above, not below. We do not get to heaven by sheer gravity. Nobody falls into heaven; we have to climb up to it.

The secret of professing our hope in Christ's promises is to believe Jesus is here in this valley of tears, precisely to enable us in coping with the trials of life and trusting that He will not abandon us. This is exactly what the Real Presence means. It means God became man, and the Incarnate God is now here with us to reassure us that we are not alone.

Perhaps the greatest terror in life is the fear of being alone, with no one to love us, care for us or help us. But Christ in the Real Presence has a real heart. His Sacred Heart beats with an unquenchable love for us. We believe Christ knows and understands and is ready to provide for all our needs on the way to heaven. He knows exactly what we need. All we have to do is come to Him, as He told us: "Come to Me, all you who labor and are heavily burdened, and I will give you rest." Nowhere in our faith is that more profoundly verified than in our faith in the Real Presence. It is as if Christ in the Eucharist is saying "That is why I am here, so that you may come to Me!"

Adoration of our Lord in the Blessed Sacrament is to include, with great emphasis, our profession of hope in Him who died on the Cross to save us from the world, the devil and our own sinful inclination. But remember: *We* must come to Him. We *must* come to Him. We must *come* to Him. We must come to *Him*. The Lord and Master of the universe is waiting for us.

BLESSINGS OF PROFESSING OUR HOPE IN THE REAL PRESENCE

The blessings we may expect are the blessings already proven by the lives of all the great saints who were devoted to the Holy Eucharist. Not only does our Lord in the Blessed Sacrament give us the courage to cope with our natural fears, He also gives us the ability to undertake great things for the sake of His name and the power to undergo great trials in our loyalty to His cause. We need the strength to undertake what the Church tells us, and we need more divine strength to undergo the trials of life.

St. Alphonsus Liguori has a delightful story in his classic work on the Holy Eucharist. He says:

After her death, St. Theresa (of Avila), who was already in
heaven, said to a nun "Those who are in heaven and those who
are on earth should be one and the same in purity and in love;
we are enjoying and you are suffering; and that which we do
in heaven with the Divine Essence, you should do on earth
with the Most Blessed Sacrament" (*Holy Eucharist*, 135).

In the last analysis, what is the reason for discouragement or dread of
not reaching heaven? It is fear of ourselves. We know ourselves too
well. We know our weakness and sinfulness and instability, and we are
all afraid. But that is why God became Incarnate and dwells with us in
the Blessed Sacrament—that we might look confidently to our heavenly home and trust peacefully in the strength that only He, our
Eucharistic Lord, can give us. This is the abundant blessing found in
coming to our Lord in the Blessed Sacrament and professing our hope
in His Real Presence in the Holy Eucharist.

P R A Y E R

Eucharistic Heart of Jesus, I believe You are truly present under the sacramental veils of the Holy Eucharist. My faith is the foundation of my hope.
My faith is the confidence of my hope. Without seeing You with bodily
eyes, I sincerely believe that You are here. Because I believe in Your Real
Presence, I also trust in Your loving mercy. I hope that You will grant me
everything that You have promised. But on one condition, that I do not
waver in my hope. Amen.

16

THE REAL PRESENCE: PROFESSION OF LOVE

Why did Christ institute His Real Presence in the Eucharist? For our profession of faith, hope and love. This chapter will focus on our profession of love.

WHAT IS DIVINE LOVE?

Surely, no single monosyllable is more common in the literature of the human race than love. By now, there are as many meanings of love as there are human beings. But what does love really mean? To love means to will good to or for someone, *velle bonum aliquis*. It means to please someone either by sharing with that person what one possesses or by doing something which is genuinely helpful.

Basically, there are two kinds of love. They are not mutually exclusive, but they are distinctive. With self-interested love, I love another person, but for my own sake—for my sake as something useful or pleasant: "I love you. You are good to me. You satisfy me." But there is another love much higher, the love of friendship. With this love, I have a selfless love for another person, for *that* person's sake, for his or her good. To please that person is a love of benevolence.

But how is divine love different from human love? Human love is the love of human beings, with human motives and in a human way. Divine love is the love for God and the love for others in a *divine* way, with our love for God being the spiritual motive.

What is divine love for God Himself? When we say divine love is the love of God, we include both levels of loving God. Firstly, self-interested (but not selfish) love of God is really the virtue of hope. Indeed, we love God, but we love Him with the expectation He will reward us for our love by blessing us with His gifts in this life and with the gift of Himself in the life to come. Secondly, totally selfless love of God is more than just a higher degree of the self-interested love. It is really an elevated, higher kind of love. It means I love God, not precisely because I expect to be rewarded for my love, but because God is so good, so great, so lovable in Himself that I want to please Him and do whatever He wants, just because He wants it and not because I will get anything from Him in return. The highest form of love for God is loving Him without looking for or expecting any recompense.

One of the best expressions of this love of God was expressed by St. Francis Xavier. The translation of this poem was by Gerard Manley Hopkins. It is worth quoting in full.

> O God, I love Thee, I love Thee—
> Not out of hope of heaven for me
> Nor fearing not to love and be
> In the everlasting burning.
> Thou, Thou, my Jesus, after me
> Didst reach Thine arms out dying,
> For my sake sufferedst nails and lance,
> Mocked and marred countenance,
> Sorrows passing number,
> Sweat and care and cumber,
> Yea and death, and this for me,
> And Thou couldst see me sinning;
> Then I, why should not I love Thee,
> Jesus, so much in love with me?
> Not for heaven's sake; not to be
> Out of hell by loving Thee;

Not for any gains I see;
But just the way that Thou didst me
I do love and I will love Thee:
What must I love Thee, Lord, for then?
For being my king and God. Amen (*For Jesuits*, pg. 9–10).

Divine love includes love for others. It means that we love others because we love God. We must stress that this is always the basis for the love of others. Genuine love for others flows from our love of God. It expresses our love for God, puts into practice our love for God and proves our love for God.

Finally, as with faith and hope, divine love is impossible without divine grace. Divine love is supernatural love and is impossible to practice naturally. It must be nourished and sustained by the grace of God. In fact, divine love does not even begin to exist unless it first has been touched by grace. Christ's statement at the Last Supper, "Without me you can do nothing," (John 15:5) is especially true when it comes to divine love. Nowhere is this statement more real than when it comes to loving God as He wants to be loved. We cannot do it without Him. It can only be done with the divine grace which comes from Christ as God and through Christ as man. Call this the alphabet of faith, but we have to explain what this alphabet is before we use it to penetrate more deeply into the mystery of the Holy Eucharist.

WHEN *MUST* WE PROFESS OUR LOVE?

We must profess our love for God whenever there is a question of divine law binding under the penalty of sin. These two words should always go together: law and love. The basic obligation of every human being is to love God by doing what He tells us we must do. We see immediately that professing our love for God is not merely verbal profession, telling God "I love you." Of course, this verbal profession should be made, but it cannot stop there. I profess my love for God when I do the will of God. That should be burned into the mind of every human being. It is what Christ told us when he said, "If you love me, keep my commandments."

Among the commandments God Incarnate gave us, one stands out with blinding clarity. In Christ's own words it is His commandment which He called the New Commandment. It is the *one* commandment by which we show, and others can recognize, that we are His followers—we must love one another, even as He who is God has loved us. That is why God became man—that He might be able to show His love for us by suffering and dying on the Cross out of love for the creatures He need not have even created or sustained. It should be stressed that this practice of Christian charity toward others is a commandment. It is our obligation and no mere option. This is where Christianity is elevated out of sight beyond all the religions of mankind. (In my years of teaching comparative religion, I have always told my students Christianity is higher than any religion in making the love of others a commandment on which our salvation depends.) In the language of the world, many people distinguish between practicing justice and charity as though justice were mandatory and charity optional. That is all right if you are a Hindu or a Buddhist, but not if you are a Christian. It is true that justice is binding, but even more binding is charity.

WHEN *SHOULD* WE PROFESS DIVINE LOVE?

The immediate answer is easy. We should profess our divine love whenever divine grace inspires us to do so. This will differ with different people. Even with the same person, it will differ at different times and different occasions as the circumstances provide the opportunity for loving God beyond the call of duty. Thus, God will give some people the grace of a vocation to the consecrated life or the priesthood or a life of virginity in the world or of dedicated widowhood. God also will put into our lives certain persons who are a special trial or burden. These so-called "burdens" are divine invitations to profess our love of God beyond what, absolutely speaking, would be necessary to keep out of sin.

To discover the difference between professing our love for God as a duty and our love for God as generosity is to have come upon a great treasure. It is the treasure of sanctity; it is the secret of holiness. It is the foretaste of heaven on earth. In the down-to-earth order in which we live, it is here especially that the petition of the Lord's Prayer is being so constantly verified when we ask, "Thy will be done on earth as it is in heaven." In heaven, everyone loves everyone selflessly, and the nearest thing to heaven on earth is for human beings to love one another selflessly.

HOW *DO* WE PROFESS OUR LOVE IN THE REAL PRESENCE?

This is the hub of our prayerful reflection. What does it mean when we say we profess our love for God in the Real Presence? We mean any one or all of the following three "P's": prayer, practice and promotion.

Prayer. We profess our love for God in the Real Presence when we come to pray before our Lord in the Blessed Sacrament. This will mean telling our Lord with our lips, and especially in the depths of our hearts, that we love Him. What follows is crucial to understanding what we are saying. Remember in Matthew's Gospel when Christ said, "You shall love the Lord your God with your whole heart, with your whole soul and with your whole mind" (22:37). Christ added the closing words "with your whole mind" because the God whom we are to love is the God who became man. We are to love this God become man with our whole mind believing with the intellect that Jesus Christ is God, that Jesus Christ our God became man and that Jesus Christ the God–man is on earth in the Blessed Sacrament. If we believe in His Real Presence, we will naturally want to come to Him in the Eucharist, professing our love for Him with our minds in prayer.

Practice. We also profess our love for God in the Real Presence by putting into practice what we profess with our lips or even profess in the depth of our hearts. Remember what we have already said? Our love for God is to be lived. It is to be lived in the real world in which He has in fact placed us—real circumstances, real conditions, real people, at the present time—so that we are putting into practice what we may be sincerely telling our Lord in prayer. Prayer before the Blessed Sacrament, we may say, is the soul of our love for God. But to be alive, a soul must have a body. The body of this soul is the active expression of what it professes in the thoughts, desires and sentiments. Finally, we profess our love of God in the Real Presence when we promote our hearts.

Promotion. Devotion to Christ in the Blessed Sacrament is made according to the limits of our state of life and the opportunities Divine providence places in our lives. We can become apostles or missionaries of the Real Presence, by promoting faith in His Presence on earth in the Blessed Sacrament. This is so important today. We live in a world which is immersed in selfishness, even to the point of cruelty with millions of people being mercilessly destroyed. How this world needs to discover the truth that *God* is love, that God who is love became man, and that this God who is love and became man died on Calvary and is on earth today. We believe this Love who became man is still on earth in the Blessed Sacrament in order to allow us an opportunity to show how much we love Him, and to obtain from Him what He alone can give us: the ability to love in a loveless world.

BLESSINGS OF PROFESSING OUR LOVE IN THE REAL PRESENCE

The great blessings which come from fervent faith in the Real Presence and faithful prayer before the Blessed Sacrament is the gift of opening the human heart to give itself to God. Of ourselves, we are all naturally self-centered, self-preoccupied, self-interested and self-opinionated. We are all naturally self-concerned, self-indulgent, self-satisfying, self-admiring and self-attentive. In a word, we are all profoundly and deeply self-willed. There is one idolatry to which every human being is constantly prone, and that is the worship of oneself.

Yet we know, on faith, that selfish people will not reach heaven. We also know from faith and experience that selfish people are not really happy. What, then, is the secret of acquiring selflessness? The secret is to obtain the light and strength we need to win the one war in which we are all engaged—the war against self. Self-conquest is impossible by ourselves. We need the grace that only Christ can give, and that is why He is on earth, present in the Holy Eucharist. That is why Love became man—so that Love Incarnate might enable us to become like Him in selfless love for Him and for all those whom He puts into our lives.

P R A Y E R

LORD JESUS, NONE OF US HAS ANY ILLUSION OF WHAT IT REALLY MEANS TO LOVE YOU. TO LOVE YOU MEANS TO LOVE WHAT YOU WANT. YOU TOLD US YOU WANT US MAINLY AND CONSTANTLY TO LOVE YOU BY LOVING THOSE WHOM IN YOUR MYSTERIOUS, UNEXPLAINABLE PROVIDENCE, YOU HAVE PLACED INTO OUR LIVES.

DEAR JESUS, WE HAVE ALL LIVED LONG ENOUGH TO KNOW WE CANNOT DO THIS WITHOUT YOU. THAT IS WHY YOU ARE HERE WITH US, NEAR US, CONSTANTLY AVAILABLE TO US, SO THAT WHEN WE COME TO YOU BEGGING FOR YOUR HELP, YOU ENABLE US TO DO WITH YOUR GRACE WHAT IS IMPOSSIBLE FOR US TO DO BY OUR OWN SELF WILL. DEAR JESUS IN THE HOLY EUCHARIST, ENLIGHTEN OUR MINDS SO THAT WITH EVERY HUMAN BEING WHO ENTERS OUR LIVES, WE WILL SEE YOU TELLING US, "LOVE ME." BY LOVING THOSE WHOM YOU PLACE INTO OUR LIVES, WE MIGHT MORE DEEPLY LOVE YOU. AMEN.

17

THE REAL PRESENCE: IMITATION OF CHRIST

Imitation of Christ. This is the final area of reflection on why Christ instituted the Real Presence. We have already seen that He gave us the Blessed Sacrament to communicate His graces to us and to give us the opportunity of professing to the Lord our faith, hope and love.

But there is one more profound reason why God became man and remains man on earth in the Blessed Sacrament. He did so and He does so in order that we might imitate Him. In the following chapter, we will examine the specific virtues which Christ wants us to imitate in His Real Presence. In this chapter, we will first ask some basic questions:

- Why did God become man?
- How are we to imitate Christ as He lived during His visible life in Palestine?
- How are we to imitate Christ as He is now present in the Holy Eucharist?

WHY DID GOD BECOME MAN?

As we have discussed more than once, God became man that He might, as the God–man, regain the human race by His passion and death on Calvary. We speculate if we ask whether the Incarnation would have taken place if man had not sinned. Maybe yes, maybe no. But we are certain that God indeed became man and that He did have a body which did die and a human will with which He did tell His Father, "Not my will, but thine be done." This is the first and elemental reason for the Incarnation—our redemption.

But we know that our redemption is not some automatic effect which Christ produced in spite of us or independent of our cooperation. Christ did indeed win for us all the graces a sinful human race needs to be saved. And Christ is the one and only mediator between sinful man and the heavenly Father, but we have got to do something. That is why we have a free will. The graces have been won for us, but we must have access to these graces and cooperate with Christ by using the graces we receive.

We believe the principal source of our redemptive graces is the Holy Eucharist. As we said earlier in this book, the Eucharist is a sacrament three times over: as Sacrifice Sacrament, Communion Sacrament and Presence Sacrament. But how are we to cooperate with the graces Christ is giving us? We do so by putting into practice the teachings of the Savior, such as those found in the New Testament in the Sermon on the Mount, in the eight Beatitudes, in Christ's long discourse at the Last Supper found in St. John's Gospel and in the scores of parables Christ preached. We must believe and put into practice *all* of Christ's teachings.

But is that all we have to do to cooperate with Christ's graces? No, it is not enough just to follow His teachings. We must also follow His example. We believe Christ was the living God who walked the streets of our earth. Therefore, His human actions were also the actions of the infinite God revealed in the finite humanity which God assumed. Thus, we see the necessity to meditate on the Gospels and study step-by-step how Christ lived during His visible stay on earth, so that by imitating the virtues He practices as man, we might become more and more like the God who wants to make us holy.

All the language we are using here only makes sense to those who want to become holy. What is holiness? Holiness is God-likeness, and since God has become man, holiness is Christ-likeness. All this is the essence of Christian sanctity. *The Imitation of Christ*, by Thomas à Kempis, is, after the Bible, the most widely read book in the world. Should it surprise us to find in this book the words of our Savior, "He who follows me walks not in darkness, but he will have the light of life" (1, 1, 1). By these words, our Lord tells us to follow His teachings *and* His manner of life.

IMITATING CHRIST'S VISIBLE LIFE

To imitate is to become like that which you are "imitating." St. Irenaeus, the second-century Church Father, speaks of "reduplication"— reduplicating the way Jesus lived. The way Christ spoke—the way He did not speak. The way He acted—the way He did not react. Jesus is the divine model become man, telling us "follow my example as man, and you will become more and more like me, who am your God."

How do we imitate Christ in His visible stay on earth? Here are some examples: Meditate on Christ's poverty at Bethlehem and put His example into practice as far as we can with His grace. Reflect on how for thirty years He lived a life of hiddeness at Nazareth. How this needs to be imitated by our self-displaying, proud, vain, sophisticated world! Consider His patience under duress, His kindness under provocation, His humility under humiliation, His charity under demonic cruelty. All of these are to be thought about, reflected on, then imitated in our own lives.

All the while, we are responding to Christ's directives that no one "comes to the Father except through Me," which here means through the imitation of His virtues that justify the Savior to say, "I am the way." The key word is "the." He meant "I, who am God, have assumed a human nature to show you by My way of life—the way you are to live, so that by living in this way, you will be on the way to heaven."

IMITATING CHRIST IN THE REAL PRESENCE

All that we have said so far has prepared the way for understanding how Christ not only was the way during His life in Palestine, but is also the way now in the Holy Eucharist.

Before we reflect on how we can imitate Christ in the Real Presence, let us remember what we said in previous chapters about "development of doctrine." All that we are saying in this book only makes sense if we understand that in two thousand years, the divine revelation Christ gave us has not quantitatively increased by one iota, but qualitatively has become clearer and more meaningful. Through the Holy Spirit, the Church grows in understanding the mysteries of Christianity. Among these mysteries, none is developed more meaningfully than the doctrine of the Real Presence.

Over almost two millennia of Christianity, the masters of the spiritual life have referred to the virtues which Christ not only practiced (past tense) during His first century in Asia Minor, but now practices (present tense) in His invisible and inaudible presence in the Blessed Sacrament. However, it was not until relatively recent times that the need for imitating Christ in His Real Presence in the Holy Eucharist has been brought to the attention of the Catholic faithful so sharply.

Two saints especially stand out as none before for their contribution to this Eucharistic development of doctrine: St. Margaret Mary Alacoque and St. Peter Julian Eymard. In their own ways, both saints gave great impetus to what we may now call the imitation of Jesus Christ in the Blessed Sacrament.

We must always keep our minds focused on the fact that Christ in the Holy Eucharist is present in the fullness of His humanity. And it is in His humanity that He can be imitated.

That is why God became man, that He might be "reduplicated" both in His mortal life on earth and in His glorified humanity invisibly present in the Blessed Sacrament. Therefore, when we speak of imitating Christ in the Real Presence, we are not speaking symbolically. We are not talking metaphorically. Christ is really, truly and fully present with a human nature, a human body, a human soul and a human heart. Christ in the Real Presence is the real Christ. He is present here in order not only to teach us by His illuminating grace or to move us by His inspiring grace. He is living in our midst also to show us how we are to follow Him. This understanding of the Real Presence will be important over the next three chapters as we reflect on how we can imitate Christ's humility, poverty and charity in the Holy Eucharist.

A good way to close this chapter is to quote from St. Peter Julian Eymard, where he is speaking of the Eucharist as the "Hidden God." It will serve as a prelude to the following chapters on the imitation of Christ in the Real Presence.

> We can understand why the Son of God loved man enough to become man Himself. The Creator must have been set on repairing the work of His hands. We can also understand how, from an excessive love, the God–man died on the Cross. But something we cannot understand, something that terrifies those of little faith and scandalizes unbelievers, is the fact that Jesus Christ after having been glorified and crowned, after having completed His mission here below, wanted still to dwell with us and in a state more lowly and self-abasing than at Bethlehem, than on Calvary itself. With reverence, let us lift the mysterious veil that covers the Holy of Holies and let us try to understand the excessive love which our Savior has for us (*Real Presence*, vol. 1, p 89).

P R A Y E R

LORD JESUS, REALLY PRESENT IN THE BLESSED SACRAMENT, YOU OVERWHELM OUR MINDS BY YOUR GENEROSITY. HERE YOU ARE IN THE HOLY EUCHARIST, TRUE GOD AND TRUE MAN, AND YET HIDDEN FROM THE EYES OF A BODY TO SEE YOU AND BODILY HANDS TO TOUCH YOU. BUT WE KNOW, WITH ABSOLUTE CERTAINTY THAT YOU ARE HERE. DEEPEN OUR UNDERSTANDING OF WHAT THIS MEANS. IN THE MEASURE THAT WE GRASP THE MEANING OF YOUR REAL PRESENCE WE WILL GROW IN KNOWING WHO YOU ARE, INCARNATE LOVE BECOME A HUMBLE MAN IN ORDER TO INVITE US POOR HUMAN BEINGS TO LOVE YOU, OUR GOD. AMEN.

18

IMITATION OF CHRIST IN THE REAL PRESENCE IN HIS HUMILITY

We have studied the Real Presence and the pattern for our imitation of Jesus Christ. Now we are in the position to look at three of Christ's virtues which He invites us to see in Him and emulate: the humility of Christ, the poverty of Christ and the chastity of Christ. For our first chapter on Christ's humility, we will ask three prayerful questions:

1. What is humility?
2. How does Christ manifest humility in the Real Presence?
3. How are we to imitate our Savior in His practice of the Eucharistic virtue of humility?

WHAT IS CHRISTIAN HUMILITY?

As a moral virtue, humility keeps a person from reaching beyond himself. It is the virtue that restrains our natural desire for personal greatness and instead leads us to an orderly, justified love for ourselves based on a true appreciation of our position with respect to God and neighbor. Humility is not only opposed to pride, but is also opposed to inordinate self-abjection. In other words, we are to be humble, but not humble in a sense that we fail to recognize God's gifts and use them according to His will.

The word "humility" comes from the Latin *humus*, which literally means dirt—good black dirt. But Christian humility rises far above natural humility in several ways. Christian humility is based on divine faith as revealed in the New Testament and is modeled on the humility of Christ. Without His humility, we would not have what we call Christian humility. Moreover, Christian humility is supernatural; it cannot be possessed as a virtue or practiced by anyone without the grace of God.

So what is Christian humility? The foundation of Christian humility is the Incarnation, which we may call the self-humiliation of God. In the words of St. Paul writing to the Philippians:

> Have this mind in you, which was also in Christ Jesus, who although He was by nature God, did not consider being equal to God a thing to be clinged to, but emptied Himself, taking the nature of a slave and being made like unto man. And appearing in the form of a man, He humbled Himself, becoming obedient to death, even to death on a Cross (Philippians 2:5–8).

God humiliated Himself by becoming man. He could not have become less, because the lowest rational creatures are human beings. We should also see that following Christ's example of Christian humility includes Christian obedience. Why? Because the God–man was so humble, He practiced obedience to His heavenly Father. To know that is to begin to understand what we mean by Christian humility.

MANIFESTATION OF HUMILITY IN
THE REAL PRESENCE

As we enter this subject, we are entering the field of revealed mystery. We cannot explain or even comprehend the meaning of Christian humility. We have to believe God wants us to be humble simply because God became man to practice humility. Our guides for seeing how Christ manifests His humility in the Real Presence are the saintly men and women whom the Church has raised to the honors of the altar. Therefore, we are secure in following their teaching and even using their vocabulary.

How does Christ manifest His humility in the Real Presence? By His self-abasement in the Holy Eucharist. Christ is present in the Blessed Sacrament not only without manifesting His divinity, but even hiding His humanity. Christ is present in the Blessed Sacrament without pomp or majesty. The Lord of nations and King of kings is in the Holy Eucharist totally unseen beyond the Eucharistic species. Christ is present in the Blessed Sacrament by abasing Himself through the performance of a stupendous miracle, the miracle of transubstantiation. Being God, He maintains the accidents (the physical properties) of bread and wine by surpassing the laws of nature. As the saints ask, "Who could hide the sun in a cloud thick enough to interrupt the sun's light and heat?" That would surely be a great miracle. Yet that is exactly what Christ does in the holier, more stupendous miracle of hiding Himself behind the Eucharistic veils. The all-great and almighty God, who became man in His divinity during His visible stay on earth, surpasses Himself in the Eucharist by hiding Himself even from sight as a human being.

Christ is present in the Blessed Sacrament with none of the resplendent glory He possesses as the Incarnate God. He has no angels announcing His presence and no protection from the coldness and indifference to which He is exposed, even from those who profess to believe in Him. In fact, Christ deprives Himself of appreciation even from many—too many—of those who are ordained or consecrated in His name in religious life. Christ is present in the Blessed Sacrament and allows Himself to be ignored by those who call themselves Christians. The greatest tragedy of the rise of what we call Protestantism is the loss of faith among millions in Christ's Real, Corporeal Presence in the Holy Eucharist.

We can see Christ's humility as He makes Himself present in the Blessed Sacrament at the words of one of His own creatures—at the words of consecration, even if the consecrating priest is himself unholy and perhaps estranged from God by grave sin. Christ allows Himself to be obedient and comes down on the altar the moment a priest pronounces the words of transubstantiation. This is humility!

With this, we find the one crisis in the priesthood in the Western world. Every other crisis is either a corollary or consequence. This crisis among priests is a weakening and loss of faith in their own priesthood—a loss of faith in being too proud to pronounce the words of consecration and having God obey their words and having what had been bread and wine become Jesus Christ.

We also see Christ's humility when we recognize He is present in the Blessed Sacrament in total silence. The Word of God which brought the world into existence out of nothing is silent in the Holy Eucharist. Christ is present in the Blessed Sacrament in such a hidden and humble way because He wants to make Himself approachable and available even to the lowliest child who believes in the Real Presence.

Over the years, I have given first Communion to many young children, and this has strengthened my faith immensely. Children really believe, with no doubt in their minds, that Jesus is here in the Blessed Sacrament. They believe they really receive Jesus into their hearts! We must remember how our Lord calls us to come to Him as children.

Lastly, Christ, we may say, is in the Blessed Sacrament without defense. He restrains His own divine power as the all-powerful Divine Majesty. He who is omnipotent, He who conquered sin and death, allows us to do as we will; and causes Himself to be vulnerable and helpless. He who is God waits for us in wordless, eternal submission.

IMITATING CHRIST'S HUMILITY IN
THE REAL PRESENCE

Imitation of Christ's humility in the Real Presence must be based on deep, divine faith. Naturally speaking, we are all proud—all of us. We sometimes might actually think we are humble, but we all tend to want to have other people think well of us. We all want people to speak well of us. We want people to recognize whatever talent we may have. We even want people to recognize our humility! We dread being ignored. We dread being criticized. We tremble at being corrected or reprimanded, and then we panic at the very thought of being ridiculed or despised. As we look more closely in our Lord's self-abasement in the Eucharist, we start to realize how much work we have to do. The key word in imitating Christ's Eucharistic humility is self-effacement. This self-effacement must begin in the mind. Only a humble mind can produce a humble heart.

How do we cultivate a humble mind? By not allowing our thoughts for even a moment to dwell in self-complacency. Humility begins in our minds as pride begins in the mind. When we see we are naturally proud, we realize that we often naturally, spontaneously admire ourselves. Self-admiration, self-adulation, self-adoration is the cardinal sin on which all other sins are based. Therefore, we shall become more and more like Christ in His humility if we fully recognize that without God we human beings would not even exist.

Moreover, we are so constantly prone to live by other people's estimates of ourselves. But we can become more and more like the humble Christ if, like Him, we accept not being recognized or appreciated by others. We shall become more Christ-like in humility if, like the Master, we not only accept but actually cherish humiliations. St. Bernard, a great lover of the Eucharistic Lord who lived this self-effacement in the Real Presence, said it this way:

> Humility, which humiliation teaches us to practice, is the foundation of the entire spiritual fabric. Thus humiliation is the way to humility; as patience is to peace or as reading is to knowledge. If you long for the virtue of humility, you must not

flee from the way of humiliation. For if you do not allow yourself to be humbled, you cannot attain to humility (*Letters*).

Dear Lord, need I tell how much work there is for me? If humiliation
is a normal road to humility, so obedience is the hallmark of a humble fol-
lower of Christ. St. Paul left us that memorable description of the
Incarnation: "Christ was obedient unto death, even to death on the Cross"
(Phillip. 2:8). But Christ did not have to die. He allowed Himself to be
crucified, indeed murdered, in obedience to His heavenly Father. But He
also practiced obedience to human beings, beginning with Mary and
Joseph. He completed His sacrificial obedience by submitting to the
Jewish Sanhedrin and submitting in obedience to the cowardly decree of
Pontius Pilate ordering Him to Calvary and death. Christ is obedient. That
is why He is on earth in the Eucharist. Talk about God obeying a creature!
As I never tire telling priests when I give retreats, "In humble obedience
to your word, God comes down on the altar—and you dare to be proud?"

If we are going to imitate Christ's Eucharistic humility, we must imitate His Eucharistic obedience. We too must be obedient according to
our position and state in life. We must obey other human beings who are
vested with authority over us from God. A letter published by Pope
Clement I before the close of the first century tells Christians the
importance of being obedient:

The head without the feet is nothing, and so the feet without the head are nothing. The smallest members of our body
are necessary and useful for the whole body. But all conspire
together and unite in a single obedience so that the whole
body may be saved. Therefore let the whole body be sound in
Christ Jesus and let each be subject to his neighbor according
to the position which grace bestows on each one (*Letters to
the Corinthians,* 37, 5–38, 2).

How, then, are we to imitate our Lord's humility in the Real Presence? We do so by our self-abasement and by our humble obedience following His example.

P R A Y E R

LORD JESUS, WE KNOW THAT WITHOUT YOUR GRACE WE ARE ALL VERY PROUD. WE ASK YOU, DEAR LORD IN THE BLESSED SACRAMENT, TO GIVE US THE GRACE TO BE HUMBLE IN OUR OWN EYES SO THAT HUMBLE HERE ON EARTH, WE MAY BE EXALTED IN THE WORLD TO COME. DEAR JESUS, HEAVEN IS RESERVED ONLY FOR THE MEEK AND HUMBLE OF HEART. MAKE OUR HEARTS, DEAR LORD, AS MEEK AND HUMBLE AS THINE. AMEN.

19

IMITATION OF CHRIST IN THE REAL PRESENCE IN HIS POVERTY

Imitating Christ's poverty is an open contradiction to the philosophy of the world. This world loves wealth. In affluent countries of the Western world, poverty is considered a curse and poor people are despised. The poor are pitied, while the rich are honored and respected. Those with wealth are powerful, and those in poverty are assumed to be weak. Even when people are in fact poor, by any modern socio-economic standards, they do not want to be poor. Certainly, no one in their right mind *chooses* poverty! How irrational could anyone be?

We must brace ourselves against this prevalent ideology if we are to truly imitate Christ's poverty in the Real Presence. Let us also bring to mind what St. Francis De Sales warned the followers of Christ: "To desire to be poor but not to be inconvenienced by poverty is to desire the honor of poverty and the convenience of riches" (*Introduction to the Devout Life*, 3, 16). Needless to say, this is more than a warning. It is an indictment, especially of those in the Church who are commissioned to proclaim the Gospel of Christ but are themselves not living lives of Christian poverty.

There are so many pseudo-poor people in this world. Although they profess (by vow, sadly) evangelical poverty, they somehow manage to have all the conveniences and advantages of wealth. St. Robert Bellarmine said that one of the main reasons for the loss of six whole nations to the Catholic Church in the sixteenth century and the suppression of thousands of monasteries and convents was the false profession of poverty by religious. This was the seed sown in the Western world for its secularization. I repeat this indictment for the twentieth and twenty-first century Church today.

Behind the Church's teaching on the dignity of poverty is Christ's own practice and praise of poverty during His visible stay in Palestine. In opening His public ministry, Jesus told His listeners, "I have come to preach the Gospel to the poor." In the first of the eight Beatitudes, which are the *Magna Charta* of Christianity, Jesus said, "Blessed are the poor in spirit." In describing the focus of proclaiming the Gospel, Christ declared "the poor have the Good News preached to them." It is the poor who over the centuries have listened. Rich people have deaf ears to the teachings of Christ. Yes, there are exceptions, but they are just that—exceptions.

In instructing His disciples to go out to evangelize, Christ directed them to "call the poor, the blind and the lame." Christ Himself lived a poor life. He was born in a stable, lived in poor Nazareth, a first century village, and worked with St. Joseph as a lowly carpenter. Christ admitted He had nowhere to lay His head. He lived on people's alms, never demanding a fee for His preaching and teaching about doing good. This would have been unthinkable. Imagine Christ, after preaching the Sermon on the Mount, sending His disciples to collect a fee from the people for His great lecture!

All of this and more could be said as we approach the imitation of Christ's poverty in the Real Presence. We do not imitate what we do not appreciate, and, to say the least, most of our contemporaries do not appreciate poverty; they depreciate it. In this chapter we will first concentrate on how Christ practices His poverty in the Holy Eucharist and then reflect on how we can apply that practice of poverty to our lives today.

CHRIST'S POVERTY IN THE REAL PRESENCE

As the writings of the Eucharistic saints make clear, Jesus wanted to be not only poor, but the poorest of the poor. Why did Jesus Christ choose to practice poverty? In order to reach out to the majority of the human race, which is poor in worldly possessions. Most of the human race goes to bed hungry every night. Hundreds of millions of human beings do not even have a bed to sleep in. A woman coming back from India once told me, "I would pull the blind on my window and look out. Evening would come and people were settling in for the night. As far as the eye could reach, I saw thousands of people ready to sleep on the hard rocky ground."

I was with Mother Teresa in Tijuana, Mexico, when she told me, "I have never seen such destitution in my life, even in the worst slums of India, as I see here in Tijuana, Mexico." Tijuana is within walking distance of the earthly paradise of our United States of America.

The purpose of this chapter is to wake up our consciences. Please God, wake up the consciences of bishops, priests, deacons and lay people to be concerned for the poor—not just to mouth poverty but according to your grace, to live poverty. Over my years in the priesthood, I have learned that for many sincere, honest people, faith is in the realm of poetry, like reading Keats, Shelley or Byron. Their hearts are as stimulated as they would be while listening to Beethoven. How beautiful! But nothing happens. Their lives go on unchanged. Many people like to talk about poverty. Some people show compassion and concern for the poor. That is good, but how few people really live poverty.

Why did Christ choose to live poverty? To make it clear that His Kingdom is not of this world. The wealth He promised His followers is not in money or in worldly possessions, but in the richness of God's grace here on earth and in the wealth of eternal glory in the world to come. These are true riches. God's grace on earth and eternal glory in heaven—that is reality. Everything else is fiction. No wonder ninety percent of all the reading Americans do is fiction—they are nourishing their dream life and feeding their minds with non-reality to escape and forget the real world God has created.

Every detail of Christ's visible earthly stay was planned and calculated to the minutest detail. On these terms, it is clear that God wanted to be a poor man, and not only poor, but actually destitute. As we look at Christ's poverty in the Eucharist, we see a perfect consistency between how He lived before His death, Resurrection and Ascension and how He now lives in the Blessed Sacrament. What adds to the significance of Christ's Eucharistic poverty is that He is now risen from the dead, no longer mortal, but glorious in the splendor of His victory over sin and death. If anything, Jesus is now poorer in His Eucharistic life than He was during His mortal life on earth.

Here, I would like to paraphrase a thought from St. Peter Julian Eymard, whose genius in describing Christ's Real Presence is incomparable. What is Our Lord's state of "wealth" in the Holy Eucharist? His home in the Eucharist may be only a poor church, perhaps worse than the cave of Bethlehem. I do not have to say how some modern Catholic churches in affluent countries do not even look like churches anymore. His home, His dwelling place, is the tabernacle. In so many poverty-stricken places around the world, the tabernacle only consists of four worm-eaten boards of wood and a lid. He lives in whatever house we provide—wherever we put Him. Talk about the helplessness of Christ's poverty!

We should always associate Christ's infancy, His speechlessness and his total dependence in Bethlehem with His condition now in the Holy Eucharist. Christ in the Blessed Sacrament brings nothing from heaven except His own adorable and invisible person. If the poor are without honor, Jesus in the Eucharist is without glory.

Many of the poor have very few friends or none at all. The homeless in New York City walk around with plastic bags across their shoulders, begging from strangers. They dress in rags and sleep on sidewalks or in holes in alleys. Many will freeze or starve to death during the severe nights. Within sight of the beautiful skyscrapers of the wealthiest nation in the world, they live and they die without notice.

In the Eucharist, Jesus also has very few friends. He is a stranger, unknown to the majority of Americans, who may walk past a Catholic church or chapel for years and never for a moment give a single thought to who is present there. He is even unknown to many Catholics! We have such a responsibility to make this Jesus Christ known by those among whom He lives and those who do not even know He exists.

IMITATION OF CHRIST'S POVERTY

As we begin to look at ourselves and how we should imitate Christ's poverty, we should distinguish between Christ's actual poverty of need and His spiritual poverty of detachment. Both are practiced by the Savior, and both are to be imitated by us. The distinction is not subtle, but crucial to a correct understanding of the Real Presence.

Actual Poverty. How do we imitate Christ's actual poverty? By being satisfied with less rather than with more of this world's goods. The more the world offers us, the more opportunities we have to imitate Christ because there is more we can give up or sacrifice!

We should imitate Christ's actual poverty by genuine poverty in the poverty of want. Poor people lack what rich people have. I remember my moral theology teacher back in the seminary telling us, "When you become priests and preach at a parish, especially a wealthy parish, you must tell the people that we all must practice poverty or we will not go to heaven." If we are going to follow Christ in His poverty, we must lack. What an examination of conscience Americans would have to make! So many Americans lack nothing. They have everything when it comes to worldly goods.

When seeking role models, actual poverty looks not to those who possess. Actual poverty identifies physically with the poor. This is where the media have mesmerized our whole nation. We have been hypnotized into the worship of wealth. But let us consider the words of St. Bernard, "I wish to be a friend of the poor, but especially their imitator. The one is the grade of beginner, the other of the perfect, for the friendship of the poor makes us friends of kings, but the love of poverty makes us kings ourselves. The kingdom of heaven is the kingdom of the poor" (*Letters*).

We should always remember this, "The kingdom of heaven is the kingdom of the poor."

Poverty of Spirit. How do we imitate Christ's poverty of spirit? If actual poverty means deprivation, poverty of spirit means detachment of the heart from whatever this world calls good.

Poverty of spirit means poverty of desire. For the sake of others, a person may possess a certain amount of this world's goods. However his heart must not be on this world, but on the world to come. The only reason that God might have for some people to be wealthy is so that they can be generous in sharing their goods for the sake of others. The actual possession of wealth *must* be for the sake of others and not for one's self or we will not enter the kingdom of heaven. Our hearts must be detached from this world. The hardest thing on earth is for a person who is not actually poor to practice poverty of spirit. A person who actually lacks is by his very life detached—there is nothing to be attached to. But especially in a country like ours, those who are not poor have earthly possessions and want more. The challenge to wealthy people is humanly impossible to practice. I know this to be true from the many retreats I have given. Let it be known: our hearts were not made to be satisfied by anything in this world. They were made to possess God.

Poverty of spirit is also humility of spirit. Why do people desire to possess? It is not mainly for the personal satisfaction wealth or money or property may bring them. You can only eat so much. You can only make the bed so big. You can only put on so many clothes. People do not accumulate wealth just to eat more or dress more—there is a limit! The real reason is because worldly possessions bring recognition and acceptance and praise and honor. It is this strategy that the devil uses to lead people into pride and from pride into all kinds of sin.

But poverty of spirit does not seek recognition or praise. Those who are spiritually poor actually prefer not to be recognized and not to be honored. Poverty of spirit is concerned for others, is thinking of others and wants to help others. Poverty of spirit recognizes that whatever I have is a gift of God and has been given to me by God to be used for *His* greater glory and not mine, for the furthering of *His* interests and not mine, to be used according to *His will* and not mine, and to be *shared* with others, according to *His* preference, and not my preference.

The saints tell us that poverty is ennobling, enriching, powerfully apostolic, deeply satisfying and divine, seeing that when God came into the world, He was born and raised in poverty and now on earth He practices such poverty in the Real Presence. This should awaken the hearts of His followers to follow in His pathway and detach our hearts sincerely from everything in the world and set them on the only true riches, which is the possession on earth of Jesus Christ crucified and the possession in heaven of Jesus Christ glorified.

P R A Y E R

LORD JESUS, YOU ARE LIVING A POOR LIFE IN THE HOLY EUCHARIST. YOU HAVE EVERYTHING, AND YET TO LIVE AMONG US IN THE BLESSED SACRAMENT YOU HAVE DISPOSSESSED YOURSELF OF EVERYTHING. AS FAR AS THE EYES CAN SEE, YOU POSSESS NOTHING. AS FAR AS THE EARS CAN HEAR YOU DO NOT EVEN SPEAK TO US IN THE HOLY EUCHARIST. BUT WE KNOW ON FAITH THAT YOU ARE THE ALL-WEALTHY GOD WHO DEPRIVED YOURSELF OF EVERYTHING WHICH THE WORLD CONSIDERED PRECIOUS IN ORDER TO ATTRACT US TO YOURSELF. TEACH US, WE BEG YOU, TO LEARN FROM YOUR EXAMPLE IN THE BLESSED SACRAMENT TO CHERISH NOTHING IN THIS WORLD AS WORTHY OF ANYTHING, EXCEPT TO REACH YOU OUR ETERNAL TREASURE, FOR WHOM WE WERE MADE. AMEN.

20

IMITATION OF CHRIST'S CHARITY IN THE REAL PRESENCE

In this Eucharistic book, we have already reflected on the love of Christ in the Real Presence from two perspectives: the manifestation of Christ's divine love in instituting the Blessed Sacrament and the profession of our love for Him in our adoration of the Holy Eucharist. Our purpose in this chapter is more distinctive. We will look at our *imitation* of Christ's charity in the Real Presence.

What do we wish to see? We want to see what is not only distinctive but unique in Christ's practice of charity in the Real Presence which we are privileged to imitate. Following the lead of the great saintly devotees of the Holy Eucharist, we will see that the charity of Christ in the Real Presence is patient to a divine degree. We will ask two questions in this chapter: How does Christ practice patient charity in the Real Presence, and how are we to imitate His patient charity in our own lives?

PATIENT CHARITY IN THE REAL PRESENCE

Charity is not just love, it is supernatural love. It is supernatural several times over. Charity is Love Incarnate. God who is Love became man to reveal to a selfish human race this divine love. Without Christ, we might still use the word "charity." But unless God had become man in the person of the Incarnate Jesus Christ, the depth of meaning of what charity is would never be known to the human race. Love had to become Incarnate to make charity even conceivable.

Charity is the love we cannot begin to practice except through the illumination and inspiration of grace which comes from God. Charity is supernatural love which only God in human form can practice or which those whom the Incarnate God has given the light and strength to practice.

Patient charity may also be called mercy. As we have discussed in a previous chapter, mercy is love which suffers and endures. Certainly, Christ practiced mercy when He instituted the Blessed Sacrament. In fact, the Holy Eucharist cost our Lord the shedding of His Blood on Calvary as He said at the Last Supper: "This is my Body which will be given up for you." And "This is my Blood which will be shed for you." Notice that the body given up for you and the shedding of Christ's Blood was necessary for the Eucharist even to come into existence. But our concentration here is on Christ's practice of mercy as patient charity in the Real Presence.

We must note that this patient charity in the Real Presence is a distinctive kind of mercy. It is not only that Christ paid (past tense) dearly to institute the Holy Eucharist. We may also say He is presently paying dearly in the Real Presence in the Eucharist. How so? In many ways, but in none more so evidently than in the neglect of His presence on earth by so many of His alleged followers, and not only those who have never heard the Gospel. Christ's patient charity is seen in the fact that after twenty centuries, most of the human race does not even believe He is on earth.

Once more I will quote from the great apostle of the Real Presence, St. Peter Julian Eymard, who paid so dearly during his own lifetime for telling people, in his own words, "The Most Blessed Sacrament is not loved."

> Alas, it is but too true: Our Lord in the Blessed Sacrament is not loved!
>
> He is not loved by millions of pagans, by millions of . . . infidels, by the millions of schismatics and heretics who

either do not know anything of the Eucharist or have no notions about it.

Among so many thousands of creatures in whom God has placed a heart capable of loving, how many would love the Blessed Sacrament if only they knew it as I do!

Must I not at least try to love it for them in their stead?

Even among Catholics, few, very few love Jesus in the Most Blessed Sacrament. How many think of Him frequently, speak of Him, come to adore Him?

What is the reason for this forgetfulness and coldness? People have never experienced the Eucharist, its sweetness, the delights of His love.

They have never known the goodness of Jesus!

They have no idea of the extent of His love in the Most Blessed Sacrament.

Some of them have faith in Jesus Christ, but a faith so lifeless and superficial that it does not reach the heart, that it contents itself with what is strictly required by conscience for their salvation. Moreover, these last are but a handful among so many other Catholics who live like moral Pagans as if they had never heard of the Eucharist (*Real Presence*, vol. 1, 148–149).

From all biographical accounts, Peter Eymard was a very gentle man, but these are hard-hitting words! Most people do not talk this way and get away with it. Nor did he. Peter Eymard was plagued with opposition from his own clergy for the outrageous criticism, which, as we know, was animated by his deep love for our Lord in the Eucharist. There is no one so courageous, so absolutely fearless as the lover in defending the beloved. This is the kind of language Catholics need desperately to hear today. Why? Because it is the truth! Because in so many parts of the Catholic world, the Real Presence in the Eucharist is unattended, sidelined, ignored, treated as though it did not exist, demeaned and even denied. Someone somewhere needs to have the courage of a Peter Eymard and speak up to defend Jesus—to defend Divine Love who became man and is in our presence in the Holy Eucharist!

The least we can do is try to make up, call it expiate, for the widespread neglect of Christ's presence. He created a world which does not recognize that He became Incarnate and less still that this Incarnate God is on earth today living in the tabernacles and exposed in the monstrances of every Catholic church and chapel of the universe. So how does Christ practice patient charity in the Real Presence? I hope Peter Eymard helped answer our first question. We all know that there is nothing on earth more painful than love given and not returned.

IMITATING CHRIST'S PATIENT CHARITY

We come now to what is our principal reason for this chapter. How are we to imitate Christ's patient charity made manifest in the Holy Eucharist in our daily lives? Let us begin this reflection by quoting from the Collect at Mass, which scholars say dates back to the ninth century. The prayer reads:

> O God, who by the patience of Thine only begotten Son didst Thou crush the pride of the ancient enemy. Grant us, we beseech Thee, to have a worthy recollection of the things which He devoutly endured on our behalf and thus, by His example, patiently to bear our adversities.

That is the spirit with which we are to examine Christ's patient charity. Note that we are to imitate His patient charity not only as He practiced it in Palestine, but as He practices it now under the sacramental veils.

To realistically come to grips with this crucial element in our following Christ, we must first ask: What is *Christian* patience? Patience in general is a form of the moral virtue of fortitude (also known as courage). Patience enables one to endure present evils without sadness or resentment in conformity with the will of God. But *Christian* patience is far more. Indeed, Christian patience includes the fortitude in bearing present evils without sadness or resentment. Only in conformity with the will of God, and in imitation of the Son of God who became man to teach us by word and example, can we begin to know how to endure suffering and pain out of love of God. This is much more than generic patience! Christian patience is the imitation of Christ's patience for a definite purpose. What is the purpose? The purpose is the salvation and sanctification of souls. What are we saying? We are saying that in God's mysterious providence, it is mainly by our patient charity with others that we cooperate with Christ the Redeemer as channels of His grace. Patient people are apostolic people; nobody else is. That is why Christ places people into our lives who cause us pain. Remember, patience comes from the Latin *patientia*, which is simply the noun for the verb *pati*, which means to suffer. We can talk about patience, write about it, give lectures on it, but we do not have any patience unless we have some pain.

Here we touch a fundamental truth of the spiritual life. We are saying that God providentially places painful people into our lives. Let us say He provides such people in our lives. These people cause us suffering, irritation or discomfort because of their neglect, oversight, indifference or even obnoxious behavior. Remember, we cannot comprehend the mysteries of the mind of God. We can only begin to see the divinely ordained reason for this from Christ's passion and death on the Cross and His divinely permitted practice of patience in the Holy Eucharist. There is a divine logic in the practice of patience:

1. Sin brought disorder into the world and deprived sinners of the grace of God.

2. In order to expiate sin and bring redemption to sinners, God became man so that He might suffer for the salvation of an alienated human race.

3. Christ did His part. He practiced patient charity by His passion and death on Calvary. As we have also seen, He practices patient charity in the Holy Eucharist. That is Christ's side of what we call the New Covenant.

4. But we must do our part. We must cooperate with Christ's redemptive work by our own patient charity toward others as God *providentially* places them into our lives. Christ puts pain-causing people into our lives for a purpose: so we have an opportunity to fulfill our side of what we casually call the New Covenant.

In the biographies of the saints, we can trace three grades or levels of patience which we should try to practice with the help of our Eucharistic Lord.

The first level is to bear difficulties, especially those caused by others. We should do so without *interior* complaint. Avoiding exterior complaining may be good business, but it is far from real patience. True patience bears its difficulties without interior complaining as well.

The second level is to use hardships to make progress in virtue. We all want to grow in sanctity. What Christian does not? But then we look at the price tag and say, "Oh no!" The price of sanctity is patience, and the ground of patience is pain, and the principal cause of pain is people. But we can endure our hardships and pain in order to grow in sanctity.

The third level of Christian patience is not only to patiently bear but to embrace the pain others cause us without complaint, because faith tells us this is the price of growing in sanctity. The highest degree of patience for which we should all pray is to actually *desire* the Cross and the afflictions out of love of God. We should accept with spiritual joy these pains and these crosses which especially come from other people. Yes, with joy! Our whole body may be trembling and our souls may be shivering as well. But spiritual joy is joy in the will, joy that comes from the mind and knowing that I am doing the will of God.

Why? Just as we pray while making The Way of the Cross, "We adore Thee, O Christ and we praise Thee, because by thy Holy Cross Thou hast redeemed the world." We believe that by joining our sufferings in patient charity with the glorified Christ in the Eucharist, we are cooperating with Him in saving a sinful world.

P R A Y E R

LORD JESUS, YOU ARE IN THE BLESSED SACRAMENT AS THE GLORIFIED CHRIST BECAUSE YOU PATIENTLY SUFFERED AS THE CRUCIFIED CHRIST ON CALVARY. TEACH US THE HARDEST LESSON WE HAVE TO LEARN IN LIFE, THAT THERE IS NO TRUE JOY IN THIS WORLD WITHOUT THE CROSS. TEACH US TO EMBRACE THE CROSS IN OUR LIVES AS YOU EMBRACED IT IN YOURS. IF WE DO, WE SHALL NOT ONLY SAVE OUR OWN SOULS BUT THE SOULS OF COUNTLESS OTHERS WHOM WE HAVE LOVED PATIENTLY HERE ON EARTH. AMEN.

21

The Need to Understand the Church's Teaching on the Holy Eucharist

If there is one thing that should be clear from this Eucharistic book, it will be that we are to live what we believe. Throughout these chapters, we have been learning how we are to practice our faith in Christ's Real Presence in the Blessed Sacrament. However, up to this point, our reflections have been mainly concerned with our own spiritual lives. Now we turn our attention to the apostolic dimension of our faith in the Holy Eucharist: How can we become apostles of the Real Presence in the modern world?

Over the next four chapters, we will look at the following issues:

1. The need for Catholics to understand the Church's teaching on the Holy Eucharist.
2. The need for Catholics to understand how the one sacrament of the Eucharist has three levels as Sacrifice Sacrament, as Communion Sacrament and as Presence Sacrament.
3. The need for understanding how the Real Presence is fundamental for the Sacrifice of the Mass and Holy Communion.
4. The need for a program of training Catholics on these three levels of understanding the Eucharist.
5. The need for motivating priests, religious and laity to promote Eucharistic adoration.
6. The need for coordinating the practice of Eucharistic adoration on a parochial and diocesan level.

NEED FOR UNDERSTANDING THE EUCHARIST

There is no doubt that our final goal in life is to reach heaven. Our purpose in living a temporary life here on earth is to live an eternal life with God in heaven. We shall reach heaven if we have done the will of God on earth. One may ask, "How do we do the will of God?" We submit our wills to the divine will of God by enjoying what *He* wants us to enjoy and by suffering what *He* wants us to suffer.

"Say that again?"

By suffering what *He* wants us to suffer.

"Do you mean God wants us to suffer?"

Of course! But notice, only in suffering what *He* wants us to suffer.

We also submit our wills to God by removing from our lives what *He* wants us to remove. In other words, we all have certain things in our lives which God wants us to sweep out.

"Even things we like?"

Yes. And the most important clean-up we have to do is in our minds—removing from our minds what God does not want us to have there.

"But I really like these thoughts!"

But God wants you to get rid of them.

We must also sacrifice what *He* wants us to surrender or sacrifice, even though no sin may be involved. So we do the will of God by enjoying, suffering, giving up and sacrificing what He wants us to enjoy, suffer, give up and sacrifice. We must remember, however, that the will is a blind faculty. It cannot choose anything except what the mind, enlightened by faith, tells the will is desirable and therefore, chooseable. You might say the will is sitting around waiting for the mind to tell it what to do. But the mind must know from reason (especially from faith building on reason) what the will should choose. An unenlightened mind is an inactive will.

This applies directly to the Real Presence. In order for Catholics to spend even five minutes in adoration before the Blessed Sacrament, their minds must first be enlightened on the meaning and value of the Holy Eucharist. Otherwise, the human will does not move the body to kneel down before the Blessed Sacrament. The human will does not even move the body to walk into a Catholic church or chapel. Why bother? The mind must be convinced that Christ, the Son of God, *really is* here on earth in the Blessed Sacrament.

It is one thing to profess to be a Catholic; it is something else to believe in the Holy Eucharist. Faith is not in certain syllables being pronounced. Faith is in the intellect, assenting to what God has revealed— not because our minds can explain why or how something is true, but because the all-truthful God has revealed His truth. It is one thing to be a practicing Catholic. It is something much more to realize what the Holy Eucharist truly is.

At the turn of the century, Pope St. Pius X organized what has since become known as the Confraternity of Christian Doctrine. A century ago, Pius X saw the growing chaos cultivated by erroneous ideas among the faithful in so many parts of the Catholic world. He said, "Most of the evils which beset the Church and most of the problems with which the Catholic Church is plagued, are not due to bad will." That needs memorizing. He goes on, "No, they are mainly due to ignorance of Christ's revealed truth" (*Acerbo Nimis,* 1). This is the fundamental reason for this book. Needless to say, we have only begun what we need to do for the rest of our lives; we have to grow in our understanding of what we believe.

So what are we saying in this book? We are applying all the basic premises of the Church's teaching to the need for Catholics to understand the Holy Eucharist. Sometimes when I talk this way, people think, "Poor Father, he thinks he is still teaching in the seminary. This is not a class of theologians doing their doctoral studies on Catholic dogma." But this is more than an academic nicety or a school-boy's riddle. Every single member of the Church has a need and a right to the truth. We are living in the most academically sophisticated nation in the world in all of history. More than five million Americans attend college campuses every year, learning everything under the sun, and beyond the sun. They can learn the inner workings not just of molecules or atoms, but of the protons and neutrons inside the atom! But that same mind, trained to the hilt and bogged down with the weight of human knowledge, can be a vacuum when it comes to understanding what God has revealed. That is intellectual horror. We must understand our faith in order to explain it to such an intellectual, academic world.

The need for Catholics to understand the Holy Eucharist is grave, urgent, widespread and crucial. As the understanding of our faith in the Eucharist goes, so goes the Catholic Church. As the Catholic Church goes, so goes the rest of the world, because we believe the Church is the mother and teacher of all nations. Why is understanding the Eucharist so desperately needed among Catholics today? Because otherwise, the reason for Christ's institution of the Holy Eucharist will be either only minimally realized or not realized at all.

Just before His Ascension, Jesus told the Apostles two things: to make disciples of all nations and to teach them "all I have taught you." Note the two words "disciples" and "teach." This is the final mandate of our Savior to the Apostles and to all of us. We must make disciples of all nations. What is a disciple? A disciple is one who has learned, whose mind has been instructed and whose intellect has been enlightened. Then Christ told the Apostles, "teach all nations all that I have taught you." Among the truths Christ taught the Apostles, none is more fundamental than the fact that God became man, that He died for the world's salvation and that this God-become-man *is* in the world in the Eucharist.

We who see this should weep over the emptiness of so many Catholic minds which do not grasp what Christ has revealed. Is there anything more important than to know that Christ, who redeemed the world, is in the world today?

The implications are obvious. We Catholics have a divinely given duty to understand what we believe about the Blessed Sacrament. Yes, we have an obligation to grow in all the virtues, but the most basic Christian virtue is faith. If we do not grow in the faith, we will not grow in any other virtue. Growing in the faith means growing in understanding and in the intelligibility of our faith and in the meaningfulness of our faith.

Closing observation: In the *Tantum Ergo*, we sing "*praestet fides suplementum sensuum defectui,*" which means "let faith supply for what is wanting in the senses." We are asking that our believing mind may be deepened in its grasp of what our senses do not convey, that behind what our eyes can see, behind the physical properties of bread and wine, is the living God who became man.

P R A Y E R

MY EUCHARISTIC LORD, I BELIEVE YOU ARE REALLY PRESENT IN THE BLESSED SACRAMENT OF THE ALTAR. BUT HOW I NEED TO GROW IN MY UNDERSTANDING OF THIS REAL PRESENCE. UNLESS I GROW IN THIS UNDERSTANDING, I AM LIABLE TO BECOME LIKE SO MANY OF YOUR OWN DISCIPLES WHEN YOU FORETOLD THE NEED OF RECEIVING YOUR FLESH AND BLOOD IN ORDER TO REMAIN SPIRITUALLY ALIVE. BUT I HAVE NO ILLUSIONS. I KNOW THIS WILL REQUIRE EFFORT ON MY PART, STRONG EFFORT, PERSEVERING EFFORT, PATIENT EFFORT TO GROW IN UNDERSTANDING WHAT I BELIEVE. TEACH ME DEAR SAVIOR TO GRASP THE MEANING OF YOUR REAL PRESENCE. AMEN.

22

HOW THE HOLY EUCHARIST IS A TRIPLE SACRAMENT

As we near the close of this book, we are focusing on the Eucharistic apostolate. We know we cannot be apostles of the Eucharist until we ourselves understand the Church's teaching on the Holy Eucharist.

This chapter will help deepen our understanding of how the one Sacrament of the Holy Eucharist has three dimensions by being a sacrament three times over: a Sacrament as Sacrifice, a Sacrament as Communion and a Sacrament as Christ's Presence. Our approach here will be twofold. First, we will look at how the one Holy Eucharist is a triple sacrament and then examine how the Real Presence is fundamental for the Sacrifice of the Mass and Holy Communion. A new catechesis has to be developed to train priests, religious and laity in the full understanding of the Holy Eucharist as a sacrament. It is really Jesus when Mass is offered, when Holy Communion is received, and all day and all night whenever and wherever the Real Presence is reserved or exposed for the veneration of the people of God.

EUCHARIST AS TRIPLE SACRAMENT

A sacrament is a visible rite instituted by Christ to confer the grace which is signified. Throughout the centuries, Catholic Christians have recognized the Eucharist as their primary source of grace. The key to understanding how the Eucharist is a triple sacrament is to understand that Jesus is the unique channel of grace for the human race wherever He exists, in whatever way He is present, and whenever He is offered.

Sacrifice Sacrament. At the Last Supper, Christ changed bread and wine into His own Flesh and Blood and did this by a double consecration. This double consecration was the visible anticipation of His separation of Body and Blood on the Cross. From the earliest days of the Church's Liturgy, it was understood that, just as Christ did, the consecration of the bread and wine must be done separately.

The external sign of the Eucharist as Sacrifice Sacrament is the separate consecration, which signifies the separation of Christ's Body and Blood on Calvary. Just as the separation of Christ's Body and Blood on the Cross merited the treasury of graces for our redemption, so the separate consecration at the Mass is the Sacrament by which the graces won for us on Calvary are distributed to the world today. In other words, the double consecration is first of all a Sacrifice. Christ really offers Himself to His heavenly Father. But the double consecration is also a sacrament. It confers the graces of Calvary. That is why the Council of Trent was at such pains to define that the Mass is a propitiatory Sacrifice. It effectively pleads with God for the remission of our sins.

"But I thought our sins were remitted?"

Only objectively. The graces for remission were obtained on Calvary, but they need to be communicated through the double consecration of the Mass. In every Mass, Jesus pleads effectively before the Divine Mercy for the remission of our sins. As a result of the pleading of Christ we can obtain the graces He gained for us on Calvary.

Communion Sacrament. Again at the Last Supper, Christ made His Body and Blood present by His words of consecration and then gave His Body and Blood as food and drink, first to His apostles. From the earliest days of the Church's Liturgy, it was further understood that the giving of Christ's Body and Blood in Holy Communion is a powerful source of grace to each communicant.

In the early third century, St. Cyprian in Africa said, "We who are one in Christ, daily receive the Eucharist as food for our salvation" (*On the Lord's Prayer*, 18). And again, St. Ambrose in the fourth century told his people, "You should receive daily what is for your daily benefit, so live that you may deserve to communicate every day" (*On the Sacraments*, 5, 4, 25).

Presence Sacrament. After Christ's Crucifixion, Resurrection and Ascension into heaven, the early Church continued doing what Christ had done at the Last Supper through the apostles and the bishops and priests whom they ordained. They reserved the consecrated Species and preserved them in sacred vessels. They did this from the very beginning of Christianity in the first century. What was the immediate reason? To provide Holy Communion for the sick and especially for the many Christians in prison awaiting martyrdom.

But the apostolic Church believed Jesus Christ remains really present in the Holy Eucharist after the Sacrifice of the Mass has been offered and after the faithful have received Holy Communion. First, we must note that this was revealed in the apostolic Church in the first century during the period when we believe divine revelation was still being communicated to the world. Indeed, divine revelation continued from the Ascension through the time of the writings of St. Paul and the other apostles up to the death of the last apostle, St. John.

Secondly, who in their right believing mind would question that Jesus, during His visible stay on earth, was a Sacrament, a channel of grace? He was the living God, the Author of grace. That same living God who became man is on earth in the Eucharist. Thus, in the Presence Sacrament, He is not only a channel of grace, not only the source of grace, He is grace. And grace is He.

As we study the evidence of the Holy Eucharist as Sacrament on all three levels, already in the early Church, two things become clear. First, on each level, the Eucharist was assumed to be Jesus Christ—Jesus Christ offering the Sacrifice of the Mass, Jesus Christ giving Himself in Holy Communion, and Jesus Christ really present in the Eucharist after Mass and outside of Holy Communion. Second, it becomes clear that the faithful did not speculate on precisely how the Real Presence is a Sacrament, how Holy Communion is a Sacrament, or how the Sacrifice of the Mass is a Sacrament. They took it for granted.

This is important to note. It is one thing to believe something is true and something else to be able to satisfy the challenging mind in explaining precisely how it is true—in this case, precisely how the Eucharist confers the grace which is signified.

The one common element in the early Church on all three levels of the Holy Eucharist was the presence of Christ on earth in the fullness of His human nature. This was taken for granted. The early Christians held the Real Presence to be an article of faith and did not question it. Thus, there was little need for detailed explanations on *how* Christ is really present in the Eucharist.

Only later, when that presence of Jesus in the Holy Eucharist began to be questioned and then doubted, did the Church have to defend the Real Presence and explain the "hows"—as far as can be done with a mystery of faith. Keep in mind that throughout the centuries, the doubts in the Real Presence were never so widespread and so deep as they are today. Certainly, the greatest challenge of Christ's Real Presence in the Holy Eucharist is in our day. Thus, we must understand why the Real Presence is absolutely fundamental for Mass and Holy Communion.

REAL PRESENCE NECESSARY FOR MASS AND COMMUNION

The purpose of this book has been to provide a deeper understanding of the Real Presence as the basis for practicing devotion to Jesus Christ in the Blessed Sacrament. This means devotion to Him in addition to His being at Mass or receiving Him in Holy Communion. We wish to see how the Real Presence is inseparable from either the Mass or Holy Communion. In fact, without the Real Presence, there is no Mass and there is no Holy Communion.

Today we hear a lot of talk about the "Liturgy" and all kinds of elaborate ceremonial and even theatrical elements of "worship." The crowds come to receive Holy Communion by droves. As our Holy Father in his first pilgrimage to the United States told the bishops, "In the face of a widespread phenomenon of our time, namely, that many of our people who are among the great numbers who receive Communion make little use of confession, we must emphasize Christ's basic call to conversion." There is no conferring of grace in Holy Communion unless the people who receive Communion believe that the Eucharist *is* Jesus Christ and that it is Christ who offers the Mass and gives Himself in Holy Communion.

There is no Mass or Holy Communion without the Real Presence. Why not? In the Mass, we believe we have the same Sacrifice as Christ made on Calvary. But on the Cross, Christ was in His humanity, body and soul, united with His divinity. How can the Mass be the same as Calvary unless Jesus is there, really present, in the Mass with His humanity, body and soul, united with His divinity? On the Cross, His Sacrifice was bloody. Christ visibly died. How can the Sacrifice of the Mass be a re-enactment, a re-presentation of Calvary, unless it is the same Jesus who is offering Himself?

"But there is no blood in the Mass."

True. But the essence of sacrifice is not blood. The essence of sacrifice is that a human will surrenders itself to the divine will. That is Sacrifice! In the Mass, Christ has to have a human will. There would be no Mass, there could be no Eucharistic Sacrifice unless it were the same

Jesus, Body and Blood, with the same human will, offering Himself, surrendering His human will for our sins. He does so not to merit the graces for our redemption—He did that already on Calvary—but to transmit those graces of divine mercy through the Sacrifice of the Mass.

The same is true with Holy Communion. At the Last Supper, Jesus literally gave His Body and Blood to the apostles. He held Himself in His own hands, and the apostles received the living (then mortal) Jesus Christ. As we know, the Jews were scandalized when Jesus foretold what He would do with His Body and Blood, "He claims He's going to give us His Body to eat and His Blood to drink!" And they walked away. That walking away in Palestine has been a prelude for millions of people walking away ever since. At the Last Supper, after giving His apostles His own living Body and Blood, Christ told them to "do this in commemoration of Me." Having ordained the apostles priests, Christ gave them power to do what He had done and further power to transmit this priestly power on to the end of time.

It is the Real Presence of Christ in Holy Communion which makes Holy Communion a Sacrament of Christ's love. In Holy Communion, we receive the Living Jesus, who is Incarnate Love, to give us the grace to love—the grace to love Him and the grace to love even the most unlovable people whom God puts in our lives. Thus, Holy Communion is the indispensable nourishment for our spiritual life. But why? Because Jesus is really present in Holy Communion. That is the only, exclusive, absolute reason. Either we receive Him or we are not getting the grace. We are either receiving the God–man, who is Love become Incarnate, who is really present in the Holy Eucharist, who is providing us with the graces to grow in love for Christ and in our love for others because of our love for Christ—or we are receiving less than a penny's worth of not very interesting bread.

But Christ is there. We are receiving what only He can give: the power to love as God, who *is* Love. Our faith in Him who said "I am the Truth" is true. He gives Himself.

P R A Y E R

DEAR JESUS, IF WE ARE TO BECOME THE APOSTLES OF THE HOLY EUCHARIST, WHICH YOU WANT US TO BE, HELP US, DEAR LORD, TO UNDERSTAND THAT THE REAL PRESENCE IS NOT SOME ADDITIVE TO THE SACRIFICE OF THE MASS AND HOLY COMMUNION; THAT THE REAL PRESENCE IS NOT SOME AFTERTHOUGHT TO THE MASS AND HOLY COMMUNION. HELP US TO SEE, WITH THE EYES OF FAITH ENLIGHTENED BY YOUR GRACE, THAT THE SACRIFICE OF THE MASS AND HOLY COMMUNION ARE THE REAL PRESENCE.

HELP US TO SEE MORE CLEARLY THAT YOU ARE REALLY PRESENT, OFFERING YOURSELF, SURRENDERING YOUR HUMAN WILL TO YOUR HEAVENLY FATHER, NOW IN AN UNBLOODY WAY, EVEN AS YOU DID ON CALVARY BY SHEDDING YOUR BLOOD. YOU ARE NOW GIVING YOURSELF, REALLY PRESENT, IN HOLY COMMUNION SO THAT BY RECEIVING YOU, INCARNATE LOVE, WE MIGHT LOVE YOU AND LOVE THOSE WHOM YOU PLACE INTO OUR LIVES IN ORDER TO SHOW HOW MUCH WE LOVE YOU. ONLY YOU, DIVINE LOVE, CAN PROVIDE US WITH THE STRENGTH WE NEED TO LOVE, LOVE EVEN UNTO DEATH, AS YOU HAVE LOVED US. AMEN.

23

TRAINING CATHOLICS IN EUCHARISTIC DOCTRINE

We now move into the practical aspect of our reflections on the Eucharistic Apostolate: training Catholics in Eucharistic doctrine. By training, we mean both instruction of the mind and inspiration of the will. In Catholic vocabulary, training means enlightening the mind in order to motivate the will. God came into this world not as some "Divine Philosopher" but as the Divine Teacher, a teacher who wants the human race to obey the divine will of God. Thus, the purpose of Catholic training, teaching and educating is to instruct the human mind in order to motivate the human will, so that the will conforms to the will of God.

We have three questions to address in this chapter. Where are the resources for Eucharistic training? Who should provide this training? How should this Eucharistic training be given?

TRAINING RESOURCES

The resources for Eucharistic training are found basically in the teachings of the Roman Catholic Church over the centuries of her existence, beginning with the New Testament. The amount of Eucharistic doctrine could literally fill a library! Most Catholics have only the faintest idea of the ocean of the Church's teaching on the Holy Eucharist from the past twenty centuries. As we have seen, the most extensive teaching on the Holy Eucharist has been occasioned by the rise of heretical Eucharistic notions. We are currently living in the most devastatingly heretical Eucharistic age in the two millennia of Catholic Christendom.

Consequently, to find these resources, we can turn to the ocean of Catholic Eucharistic doctrine. Beneath this ocean of truth stands the authority of the Bishop of Rome. Without the successors of Peter, people today would not even know that "Eucharist" was a word. It would have died long ago, because in order to provide resources for Eucharistic teaching, we need to have recourse to:

- The General Councils of the Church approved by the Bishops of Rome.
- The regional Councils of the Church, also when and insofar as they were approved by the Bishop of Rome.
- The encyclical letters issued by the Bishop of Rome.
- The decrees and directives of the Holy See, which are always under the authority of the Bishop of Rome.

When we speak of resources, it cannot be too strongly emphasized how the teaching authority of the Vicar of Christ is crucial to ensure soundness of doctrine on the Holy Eucharist. Among the most extensive papal teachings on the Holy Eucharist in the twentieth century were the writings of Popes Pius X, Pius XII, Paul VI, and John Paul II. All the recent popes have given us a mountain of Eucharistic doctrine. But these four are especially outstanding for the sheer quantity of Eucharistic pronouncements; for the clear interrelationship of the three levels of the Eucharist as Sacrifice, Communion and Real Presence; and especially for strongly defending the revealed truth that Christ is continually present on earth in the Blessed Sacrament.

Given the rise of so many erroneous ideas, Popes Pius X, Pius XII, Paul VI and John Paul II are prolific in reiterating and clarifying and integrating the revealed truth that without the Real Presence, there is not only no Sacrifice of the Mass and no Holy Communion, but there is also no Catholic Church. Of course, a library of secondary sources has been published. For instance, if you look at just the Greek and Latin Church Fathers, you will find more than two hundred volumes containing hundreds of thousands of words on the Eucharist. However, the key for assessing these resources is always fidelity to the Church's Magisterium, which is under the authority of the Bishop of Rome.

In our own time, the publication by Pope John Paul II of the new Catechism of the Catholic Church is a major event. It is good medicine for the diseases of confusion, religious illiteracy and ignorance which are pandemic in the Church today. The Catechism is the place to start in the resources of the teaching Church. It provides answers which are clear, concise and correct.

WHO IS TO PROVIDE THE TRAINING?

We may classify those who are to provide training into three basic groups: parents training their children, priests training their people and teachers training their students. As we examine the roles of each of these groups, please keep in mind that we are talking about training, not just teaching in the academic sense.

Parents. The most influential teachers in religious doctrine are parents. This primacy of parents in the religious training of their children comes from the fact that parents are responsible before God not only for the physical, but also for the spiritual nurturing of the children they bring into the world.

But the parents' primacy is deeper still. In God's providence, parents are the primary channels of grace for their children. God wants to use parents as the generators and sustainers not only of their children's natural life, but also, with divine emphasis, their children's supernatural life. This supernatural life has a foundation, which is the faith. And within this faith, there are no fundamental truths more important than the Incarnation and the Holy Eucharist. The main purpose of being parents is not to bring children into *this* world, but to bring children into eternal life! Families are not made for this world; families are made for eternal life.

Priests. If there is one theme of Pope John Paul II, it is his insistence on the role of the priesthood for training people in the sublimity and dignity and beauty and necessity of the Holy Eucharist. If there is one Pope who will go down in history as the Pope of the Eucharist, it is Pope John Paul II. He never tires of associating the priesthood with the Eucharist. Consider these words addressed to bishops and priests:

> Through our ordination, we are united in a singular and exceptional way with the Eucharist. In a certain way, we derive from the Eucharist, we exist for the Eucharist, we are also, and in a special way, responsible for the Eucharist: each priest in his own community and each bishop, in virtue of the care of all the communities entrusted to him. (John Paul II, Encyclical On the Mystery and Worship of the Eucharist)

Religious Educators. Religious educators are to train their students in the correct knowledge, intelligent understanding and faithful practice of the Catholic faith. Within this faith, the core of its meaning and the heart of its living is the Holy Eucharist.

The Second Vatican Council published an entire document on Christian education called "Declaration on Christian Education" (*Gravissimum educationis*). In this document, the Council re-emphasized the value of schools to assist parents in the proper upbringing of their children. The Council also insisted that the schools under the Church's authority be Catholic schools. In practice, this means the religious instruction they give must be authentically Catholic. It is the essence of Catholic education to teach the unqualified doctrine of two mysteries of our faith that go together indispensably: the Incarnation and the

Eucharist. Without the Incarnation, there would be no Eucharist, and without the Eucharist, the Incarnation would not be the God–man offering Himself in the Mass, giving Himself in Holy Communion and living in our midst in the Real Presence.

HOW TRAINING IS TO BE GIVEN

Like any other form of training which involves the mind and the will, those being trained need to be instructed. Words have to be spoken. Educational materials have to be used. All the available means of pedagogy should be employed with obvious difference depending on who is doing the instruction and who is being taught. For example, a mother will not teach her child about the Eucharist the same way a priest will give a homily about the Blessed Sacrament. Also, since the Eucharist is not only to be believed but lived, Eucharistic training must provide for developing the will and emotions in order that the Blessed Sacrament may become part of a person's life.

But there is much more here. In answering the question of how people are to be trained in Eucharistic doctrine, we must remember that we are dealing with the order of grace and not only of nature. Faith in the Real Presence is a lifetime commitment. This kind of commitment requires the constant access to supernatural grace. At Baptism, we are infused by God with the supernatural powers, or virtues of faith, hope and charity. It is not sufficient to simply receive these virtues. They must be nurtured, developed and motivated through our entire lifetime by the constant influx of divine light, otherwise known as illuminating grace.

When we talk about training people in the Holy Eucharist, what we really mean is providing them with the constant pouring of grace into their minds. Books are not the answer. Classes, speeches and homilies are not the answer. These works are merely the channel or apparatus through which God confers the grace.

This is the heart of this book. Parents, priests and teachers may have all the academic knowledge in the world, but they will be useless, and in some cases positively harmful, unless they are themselves Eucharistic believers and lovers. In God's ordinary providence, He uses human beings as channels, means and conductors through which He communicates His grace for the illumination of the mind. For people to put that Eucharistic faith into practice, we must have Eucharistic parents, Eucharistic priests and Eucharistic teachers. The degree of academic training is quite secondary. The wealth of vocabulary is dispensable. What is indispensable is that we are used by Christ in order to pass God's grace on from Him, through us, and to those whom we are training.

P R A Y E R

LORD JESUS, WE WHO HAVE THE TRUE FAITH AND BELIEVE IN THE HOLY EUCHARIST ARE NOT TO KEEP THIS FAITH TO OURSELVES. WE ARE TO SHARE IT WITH OTHERS. DEAR LORD, WE CAN SHARE OUR EUCHARISTIC FAITH ONLY AS EFFECTIVELY AS WE OURSELVES ARE EUCHARISTIC BELIEVERS: BELIEVING THAT YOU WHO DIED ON THE CROSS CONTINUE TO OFFER YOURSELF IN THE SACRIFICE OF THE MASS; BELIEVING THAT WHEN WE RECEIVE YOU IN HOLY COMMUNION, WE RECEIVE THE SAME JESUS WHOM MARY CARRIED IN HER WOMB FOR NINE MONTHS; AND BELIEVING THAT WHEN WE ARE BEFORE YOU IN THE BLESSED SACRAMENT, WE ARE, AS THOMAS WAS AFTER YOUR RESURRECTION, IN THE PRESENCE OF OUR LORD AND OUR GOD. AMEN.

24

MOTIVATION FOR PROMOTING EUCHARISTIC ADORATION

As we come to the end of this Eucharistic book, we still have one more important area to prayerfully consider: the motivation for promoting Eucharistic adoration. Here we ask, "How do we convince people that Eucharistic adoration is desirable?" I use the word "desirable" advisedly because I believe Eucharistic adoration is necessary.

In order to place this chapter in context, we need to look honestly at the world situation in our day and ask, "How can the global problems of the modern world be resolved or even coped with?" The only possible response is to stand with St. Peter and answer, "Lord, to whom shall we go . . . we have come to believe and know that You are the Christ the Son of God."

THE WORLD SITUATION IN MODERN TIMES

As an objective viewer looks at the modern world, especially the Western world in countries once strongly Christian and even devoutly Catholic, the picture is clear. Speaking at the end of the special Synod called by Pope John Paul II in 1991 at Rome, the bishops drew up a statement in reference to Europe, but it also applies to America:

> In various parts of the Continent, particularly among the young, the Christian Faith is almost unknown because of the spread of atheism or wherever the process of secularization has gone so far that evangelization has to be begun almost

from the start. But even where the presence of the Church has previously been strong, only a small number take a full part in the life of the Church" (*L.O.R. 23-30, December 1991*).

The widespread de-Christianization of large parts of the Western world can be seen in many aspects of life:

- In the almost universal legalization of the murder of the unborn.
- The breakdown of family life to the point where in some countries, divorce is automatic on the request of one of the "married partners." It is too quick and easy for the marriage to be "dissolved."
- In the practice of contraception as an accepted way of avoiding the responsibilities of child bearing and child rearing, especially in affluent countries like our own.
- In the growing practice of murdering the aged and those who are suffering physical pain.
- In the corresponding legalization of suicide in more than one country.
- In the global conflict between nations. The twentieth century was the most homicidal century in human history. More people have been killed in war since 1900 than in all the wars of mankind since the dawn of recorded history.

So the record of our times goes on, and the end is not in sight. It is not likely that the twentieth century will win any prizes for beauty, goodness, fidelity or moral rectitude.

INADEQUACY OF A NATURAL SOLUTION

The more clearly we see what is going on, the more convinced we become that no natural, earthly or human means can solve the problem. What is the answer? It is the answer St. Paul gave the Roman converts in the first century, "Where sin has abounded, the grace has even more abounded" (Romans 5:20). He knew the chaotic condition of the world he lived in. Only with the coming of Christ could the chaos of the ancient world even be lived with, not to say resolved.

Surely in our day, sin has abounded full measure and is flowing over. But faith tells us that in God's providence, grace will even more abound. Remember our question: How do we motivate people to take themselves to Christ's Presence on earth today? Remind them that Jesus Christ transformed the ancient world, the world not only before Christ, but the world previously *without* Christ. Christ transformed the ancient unbelief of the Roman Empire—an Empire so ungodly that by law, no woman could give birth to a child without immediately bringing the child to the father and asking him, "Do you want this child to live or die?" That was the law. And most of the female children were killed.

Christ did it in the past; He can do it in the present. That is why I like to quote the statement of our present Holy Father, given the massive evil of the twentieth century beyond human description. Despite the ungodliness in our day, Pope John Paul II believes the twenty-first century promises to be a great renaissance in Christian history. But he keeps adding, "provided we who have the faith live it." We believing Catholics are the hope of the world. That is what the early Church Fathers told the believing Christians of their day: "You are the *anima mundi* [the soul of the world]. You are the one hope for the world coming back to life again."

Needless to say, the hope is our faith in Jesus Christ. As St. Paul tells us, "the grace has even more abounded." The grace is available, and the miracles of conversion can be expected. How? From the same Jesus Christ whose Gospel transformed the Roman Empire from pagan idolatry and moral decadence into martyrs and believing Christians. Today, St. Peter the Apostle has a successor in Rome. Caesar does not.

CHRIST THE MIRACLE WORKER ON EARTH

We are liable to overlook or minimize the signs and wonders Christ performed during His visible stay on earth. He performed physical miracles of healing and even raising the dead. But the greatest miracles He performed were the intellectual and moral miracles of belief and faith in the mind. Remember the stubborn murderer named Saul? Remember Him present at Stephen's martyrdom? He enjoyed the spectacle. But we know the miracle Christ worked in him and many of his contemporaries in a time when becoming a Christian meant becoming a martyr.

Christ promised to work even greater miracles in the future. He would work greater signs through those who would believe in Him. Today's world needs miracles in one secularized and de-Christianized culture after another. Who is to work these miracles? The same Jesus who performed them at the dawn of Christianity. That is why Christ is on earth: to work miracles for those who believe. He continues His Divine Work, especially in performing the miracles of converting stubborn, willful, proud, selfish, sex-maniacal human beings into humble, patient, chaste, obedient and generous creatures of God.

All we have been saying about the Real Presence in this Eucharistic book culminates right here. We who believe in Christ's abiding Presence in the Holy Eucharist are to become apostles of the Real Presence to our generation. We are to convince them that the almighty power of Christ to work miracles is available in our day on one premise—that we come to Him in the Eucharist and confidently beg Him to give us what we so desperately need.

Where Eucharistic adoration is practiced and promoted, the results are phenomenal, especially in the graces of conversion. Over the years, I have seen how true this is, especially ever since I was called to Rome to be told that the Holy Father desperately wants Eucharistic adoration promoted throughout the world. I have spoken to those who have seen the wonders Eucharistic adoration produces. Bishops tell me they have seen miracles, and I have no doubt. How then are we to motivate people to come to our Lord in the Blessed Sacrament and adore Him present in our midst? The strongest motivation will be our own experience in knowing what the Real Presence has done in our own lives.

P R A Y E R

Lord Jesus, I believe that You are here on earth, the same Incarnate God who performed countless miracles in Palestine. I know what miracles of conversion are needed in the world at large, and even among people who are nearest and dearest to me. I know that You are ready to work these marvels of Your mercy if only I come to beg You with a humble and believing heart. Above all, dear Lord, I know what graces I need to make me patient, humble, chaste, obedient, poor in spirit and above all, absolutely selfless in my love of those whom You have placed into my life. I am confident, my Savior, that You will make me an apostle of Your Real Presence if only I am faithful to the graces You, my Eucharistic Lord, are giving me. Amen.

25

MARY, MOTHER OF GOD, MOTHER OF THE HOLY EUCHARIST

No book on the Holy Eucharist would be complete without at least one chapter on the Blessed Virgin Mary. We know adoration is due to God alone because He alone is worthy of veneration as the source and destiny of our being. We have also seen that since God became man in the person of Jesus Christ, our adoration of Jesus is really the adoration of God in human form. Since Christ in the Blessed Sacrament is here on earth with all of His divinity along with the humanity He received from Mary, we are to adore Him. Christ in the Holy Eucharist must be acknowledged. This is the highest form of worship we can render to God and the most powerful source of grace we have on earth in our journey to a heavenly eternity. The Blessed Mother is the model of what our adoration of Christ in the Blessed Sacrament should be. In this chapter, we will cover the following topics.

- Mary, the origin of the Holy Eucharist.
- Mary, the model of our faith in the Holy Eucharist.
- Mary, the pattern of our humility through the Holy Eucharist.
- Mary, the inspiration of our patience through the Holy Eucharist.

ORIGIN OF THE HOLY EUCHARIST

When the Angel Gabriel appeared to our Lady and invited her to become "the mother of the Most High," she accepted the invitation and, as a result, she gave us the Holy Eucharist. Except for Mary there would

173

be no Incarnation, and thus there could be no Eucharist. Why not? Because the Eucharist *is* the Incarnate Son of God now on earth in the Holy Sacrament of the altar.

We are saying much more than our words might seem to imply. To say Mary is the origin of the Eucharist is to say that she, by the voluntary acceptance of her divine maternity, was (past tense) the origin of the Incarnation. Since the Eucharist is the Incarnation continued on earth today, Mary is (present tense) the origin of the Holy Eucharist. This tells us volumes on the power of Mary's free will. We are so aware of the devastation man's free will can perpetrate: nations destroyed, millions of babies killed in abortion, and the breakdown of family life on the scale never before conceived in human history. We can be so over-whelmed by the awful power of the human will to perpetrate evil that we need our Lady to see how much that same human free will can achieve or accomplish when the human will submits itself to the divine will. The greatest power in God is His free will. The greatest power in man is his free will. This is power to do evil and power to do good. Mary's voluntary acceptance of God's will made the Incarnation and thus the Holy Eucharist possible. The Real Presence is a reality because Mary used her free will. She chose to do what was more pleasing to God. She said yes to the message of the angel.

MODEL OF FAITH

The Blessed Mother lived in such physical proximity and loving inti-macy with her divine Son as uniquely as anyone could hope to experience. She carried Him in her womb for nine months. She nursed Him. She bathed Him. She clothed Him. She took care of Him in His infancy. She was with Him, near Him and close to Him physically and emotionally as only a loving mother can be close to the child whom she brought into the world. Mary was always thinking of Jesus.

Yet, all the while, what did she see in Bethlehem? A helpless Infant. A growing Child. A young Man. That is what she saw with her bodily eyes. But what did she believe? She believed that this Infant, this Child, this young Man was no mere human being. She knew He was human, but she believed in His divinity because her mind penetrated beyond the veils of what her eyes and ears and hands could experience. Faith penetrates. Faith sees. Faith knows what the senses cannot perceive and even the human reason cannot comprehend. The Church speaks of the *Lumen Fidei*, the Light of Faith. Mary saw. It cannot be too strongly emphasized or too often insisted that Mary had to live by faith. She saw only a helpless, speechless baby, yet she believed He was the Almighty Word of God.

This is the first foundational lesson we learn from Mary in our veneration of the Holy Eucharist. Like her, we must come before the Blessed Sacrament with total undiluted faith. We believe that which the pagan, sophisticated, over-educated world tells us is a dream. When we come before the Blessed Sacrament, we need to break through the crust of what the senses perceive and what the mind rationally would tell us, believing more than we can see, believing more than we can touch, believing more than we can experience with our senses or even fathom with our minds. This is why we speak of our Lady as the model of our faith. "O Mary, Virgin most faithful, pray for us that our faith may become more and more like yours."

MODEL OF HUMILITY

The Blessed Virgin Mary is the pattern of our humility through the Holy Eucharist. If there is one virtue that Mary practiced to an eminent degree, it was the virtue of humility. At the Annunciation she told the angel, "Behold the handmaid of the Lord." In the *Magnificat*, she repeated the same term except she spoke of the lowliness of His handmaid to make sure nobody misunderstood what she meant by "handmaid." She told of how the Lord scatters the proud and exalts the lowly.

There are two kinds of exaltation: self-exaltation and divine exaltation. The greatest danger on earth is self-exaltation, because then we call down on ourselves the curse of God. But the condition for divine exaltation is lowly, Marian humility. She declared that the Lord fills the hungry with good things. Those who admit their emptiness hunger, and in the Bible, hunger means emptiness not only of the body, but a symbol of the admitted emptiness of everything. By ourselves, we are empty. We are a vacuum. But we must admit that we are a vacuum, or we shall not be filled by the goodness of God. We must admit and constantly confess our emptiness, which is another word for humility.

Mary declared how grateful she was that the Lord had done so much for Israel and His servant. Humility serves. Humility waits on others. Humility responds to the bidding of the one whom it serves. This is the Mother of God, but only because she is also the lowly handmaid of the Lord. The more gifted a person, the more prone that person is to pride. Possession of anything naturally generates pride. Not only does possession generate pride, but the greater the possession, the more pride it generates. Wealth of any kind inflates the human heart. The more a person has of physical, mental, moral or even spiritual riches; the harder it is for that person to be humble. How are we to be humble? How can we possess without being proud? Only through being in the presence of Jesus Christ.

Throughout this Eucharistic book, we have looked at the unspeakable humility of God not only as in the Incarnation when He appeared as man, but also in remaining on earth in the Holy Eucharist. This is double humility: the humility of hiding His divinity as He did during His visible stay on earth and the divine humility in hiding even His humanity in the Holy Eucharist. He not only gives us the example of how humble we should be, but through Him, we receive the most funda-mental grace we need in life: the grace of humility.

Remember what we have said. No matter what we possess, it tends to induce us to pride, and the more we have, the more tempted we are to be proud. It is not just quantitative possession; it is qualitative posses-sion that inclines to pride. The highest possession we can have is sanctity. Dear God, how can I stay humble and grow in sanctity? This was the greatest temptation of the mystics. You do not possess the close union with God that saints like Catherine of Siena or Theresa of Avila or John of the Cross enjoyed without being tempted by pride. It is tempting to look down on "those lower mortals."

But Mary's humility is a paradox. The most gifted creature ever pro-duced by the Creator was also the lowliest in her own eyes. Thus, the key to humility is seeing our own lowliness: seeing everything we are, every-thing we have, everything we hope to become, everything we hope to achieve or possess—seeing everything as a free, undeserved and totally gratuitous gift from God. This is possible only by the grace which the God who became man gives us. The same grace He provided Mary by His Real Presence with her, He provides by His Real Presence with us today. There is no more basic reason for the Real Presence on earth of Jesus Christ than to provide us with the humanly impossible grace of humility.

MODEL OF PATIENCE

The Blessed Virgin Mary is also the inspiration of our patience. As we know, patience is the voluntary acceptance of suffering. There must be suffering. There must be acceptance. But the acceptance must be voluntary.

Mary lived a life of constant patience: patience not only of present suffering, but patience with anticipated suffering. This was the patience of love. She suffered by anticipation when Simeon told her a sword would pierce her heart because her Son would be rejected and persecuted by His enemies.

Mothers have told me there is nothing more painful to them than to see their children suffering. As the Church over the centuries has been telling us, Christ underwent His passion, and Mary underwent her "compassion," suffering with Him. She suffered interiorly when she had to flee with Jesus to Egypt because the murderous Herod wanted to kill her Son. She suffered when she lost her Son for three days. She suffered during Christ's public ministry when she saw Him opposed, maligned and hated viciously by those who envied His success. Mary suffered during Her Son's unjust condemnation to death. Tradition tells us she followed Him on His Way of the Cross, and the Scriptures tell us she stood on Calvary as He bled to death on Good Friday.

We need Mary's inspiration, not just to suffer, but to suffer willingly, uncomplainingly, generously and most of all, lovingly. Why? Because like Mary, we love the One for Whom, with Whom and from Whom we are suffering. Here she teaches us one of the most important lessons about the faith we need to know. She teaches us by example how we can suffer willingly, uncomplainingly, generously and lovingly. We can do so only as Mary was able to suffer what she suffered, patiently, drawing strength from the presence of Jesus Christ. He was on earth near her and with her. He is on earth now near us and with us.

When we think of how it all began, we, like Mary, must believe. We must believe that the One who is right next to us in the Holy Eucharist is our God. We also believe that to those whom Christ loves the most, He offers the opportunity for the deepest and most agonizing pain. That is our faith. Love is shown by pain. Love is proved by pain. Love lives on the patient endurance of pain. Why? Because that is what love is. We need the strength to suffer patiently. Where did Mary get her strength? From her Son, with her and near her. Where do we get our strength to suffer patiently? From Mary's Son, with us and near us. He is present in the Holy Eucharist as the all-powerful God, giving us the strength we need to suffer and to love Him more. He gives us the privilege of suffering with Him, like His Mother.

The Holy Father hopes the worship and adoration of the Holy Eucharist will be promoted and practiced in every nation because, in his judgment, it is the only possible hope for bringing a mad world back to its senses. That is why for the first time in the history of Catholicism, Pope John Paul II has ordered Eucharistic exposition all week in St. Peter's Basilica, and that is why he has placed a religious community of women there all day and every day. When the Holy Father inaugurated this historic practice of perpetual Eucharistic adoration, he pronounced a prayer I would like to substantially share with you.

Before sharing this prayer, he addressed our Lord in the Holy Eucharist by saying, "Hail, O True Body, born of the Virgin Mary, which really suffered and was sacrificed on the Cross for mankind."

— Prayer of Pope John Paul II —

"Lord, stay with us. These words were spoken for the first time by the disciples of Emmaus. Subsequently, in the course of the centuries, they have been spoken an infinite number of times by the lips of so many of Your disciples and confessors, O Christ. As Bishop of Rome and first servant of this temple which stands on the place of Peter's martyrdom, I speak the same words today. I speak them to invite You, O Christ, in Your Eucharist, present to accept the daily adoration continuing through the entire day in this temple, in this basilica, in this chapel. Stay with us today and stay from now on, every day according to the desire of my heart which accepts the appeal of so many hearts from various parts, sometimes far away, and above all, meets the desire of so many inhabitants of this Holy See. Stay that we may meet You in the prayer of adoration and thanksgiving, in the prayer of expiation and petition to which all those who visit this basilica are invited. Stay." (Excerpted from "'Lord, stay with us!' : Pope John Paul's Prayer in the Blessed Sacrament Chapel," Dec. 2, 1981, L'Osservatore Romano, Dec. 14, 1981, pp. 10–11.)

In the years since the Holy Father inaugurated Eucharistic exposition in St. Peter's, devotion to the Real Presence has grown beyond all expectations.

26

THE SACRED HEART IS THE HOLY EUCHARIST

Devotion to the Sacred Heart of Jesus goes back to the early Church in the time of divine revelation. Like all other true devotions in the Catholic Church, devotion to the Sacred Heart is based on divine revealed truth.

Two passages in Sacred Scripture are the revealed foundations for the Sacred Heart devotion. The first is Christ's invitation to His followers, "Learn from me, for I am meek and humble of heart." The second revealed foundation is Christ's Sacred Heart being pierced on the Cross by the soldier's lance. From the very beginning, the followers of Christ were devoted to the Heart of Jesus. Our focus will be on what we mean when we say the Sacred Heart *is* the Holy Eucharist. Then, we shall discuss why this is so and how we can put Sacred Heart devotion into practice.

THE SACRED HEART *IS* THE HOLY EUCHARIST

Why do we make this equation? What do we mean when we say the Sacred Heart *is* the Holy Eucharist? We begin by recalling the centuries of Church teaching on what the term "Sacred Heart" expresses. The Sacred Heart signifies Christ's love in three ways: God is love, God is loving and God loves with human feeling.

God is Love. The Sacred Heart symbolizes the love that is God. From all eternity, God is love. That is the primary meaning of God as a Divine Community and not a single Person. The essence of love is to give, and within the Trinity, each of the three Divine Persons from all eternity share the divine nature which each one possesses. When we say God is love, we are defining God as that Community of three Divine Persons who, from all eternity, each share with the other the fullness of what each one not only has, but of what each one *is*.

God is Loving. God is loving not only by bringing us into being, but by bringing us into being as creatures who are capable of love. God could have made us insects or animals or trees or lofty mountains, but these cannot think and love. When this loving God chose to create other beings, it was only because He is loving that He wanted to share what He as God had from all eternity (love) with beings who would not even exist without His love. From the moment of creation and into the endless reaches of eternity, God will continue loving us. If He were to cease loving us, we would cease to exist! God manifested His love by bringing us into existence and making us creatures who are capable of love.

But God also manifested His love by becoming one of us, and having become one of us, He has remained and will be for all eternity one of us. When the Word became Flesh, It became Flesh not only for time, but for all eternity. God will remain Incarnate forever. This loving God, who out of love for us became man and died on the Cross to show His love for us, this God became man and remains man, but He remains man on earth.

It is no exaggeration to say that the Sacred Heart *is* the Holy Eucharist. The Eucharist is the same Infinite Love who is God and who out of love for us became man and is here on earth. When we receive Him, that same God is within us. Love wants to be intimate. Love wants to be near. Love wants to be close to the one whom it loves. The Holy Eucharist is divine genius!

God Loves with Human Feeling. The third meaning which the Church gives to the Sacred Heart as symbolizing God's love is that God loves not only as God but also as the God–man with human feeling, human emotion, human sensibility and human sensitivity. We creatures of feeling, emotion and sensitivity need to hear this. God in the Holy Eucharist is man indeed, but with all the supreme sensitivity. Christ in the Blessed Sacrament is a sensitive Christ. He feels. St. Margaret Mary tells us that Christ in the Eucharist senses in a way we as hypersensitive human beings can understand.

Wives tell me, "I spend hours cooking the meal and all my husband does is sit down, eat and even ask for more. But he never thanks me!" Or among religious, "Father, you have no idea how much it hurts me to know that when we pass in the corridor, he does not even look at me." How sensitive we are! How we need to know that God became a sensitive human being! When we come to Him in the Blessed Sacrament, He wants us to tell Him how we feel, and He will tell us how He feels. When we come to Church, we should not leave our heart in the car. When Christ came to earth, He did not leave His Heart in heaven.

WHY IS THE SACRED HEART THE HOLY EUCHARIST?

It is impossible to identify the Holy Eucharist too closely with Jesus Christ. We should remember He is in the Holy Eucharist not merely with His substance. I have corrected many of my students over the years who tell me, "Transubstantiation means that the substance of bread and wine become the substance of Jesus Christ." I reply, "No, transubstantiation means the substance of bread and wine are no longer there. The substance of bread and wine is replaced not only by the substance of Christ's Body and Blood. What replaces the substance of bread and wine is Jesus Christ!" Everything that makes Christ, Christ replaces what had been the substance of bread and wine. The substance of bread and wine become the whole Christ.

Therefore, Christ in the Holy Eucharist is here with His human heart. Is it a living heart? Yes! That is why the revelations our Lord made to St. Margaret Mary about promoting devotion to the Sacred Heart were all made from the Holy Eucharist.

Why do we equate the Sacred Heart with the Holy Eucharist? Because the Holy Eucharist is the whole Christ with His human heart. According to St. Margaret Mary, the Sacred Heart *is* the Holy Eucharist. So it follows that devotion to the Sacred Heart is devotion to the Holy Eucharist. It is infinite Love Incarnate living in our midst in the Blessed Sacrament.

PRACTICING SACRED HEART DEVOTION

How do we practice devotion to the Sacred Heart? The answer to this question is almost too obvious to express, but it is the most difficult task we have in life. We are to love Him in the way He *has been* loving us and in the way He *is presently* loving us.

First the past. How has God been loving us? He brought us out of nothing into existence, making us human beings with minds to think and wills that can choose. Then, God became man and died out of love for us. We should note how these two words go together: love and death. True love wants to exhaust itself out of love for the one whom it claims to love. That is why God took on a human nature: so that He could manifest to human beings in the strongest language accessible how deeply He loves us. In the person of Jesus Christ, God died out of love. We know that if we love, we will die for the one whom we love; and the death of the body is only a symbol of the constant death of the human spirit, surrendering itself to God's will.

Next, how is God presently loving us in the Holy Eucharist? By totally giving Himself! If during Mass, I notice the cross on the consecrated Host is not quite straight, I may move the Host a quarter of an inch. That is Love allowing Itself to be moved. I am speaking from my heart. At the same time, God is constantly and lovingly pushing, shoving, shifting and nudging us. He wants us to change. He wants to move our wills, even if we remain statuesque.

How are we to return this love that Christ had for us and presently has for us? By totally and constantly conforming, submitting and surren-

Sacrifice God wants of us during
r wills. God has given us a free
ld not love. God never coerces us
selfless love of us. He invites us
and sacrificing our wills to His.
ur wills.
mean just that: giving up! We can
in doing it. Deep down inside we
ive up our wills completely and
we must say, "Lord, I will do what
but Yours." Every moment of our
God's love for us, inviting us to
ourselves.

31776 **Autom** Y E R

, INFINITE LOVE, WHO BECAME MAN. WE BELIEVE YOU, WHO ARE GOD'S LOVE INCARNATE, NOT ONLY BECAME MAN, BUT ARE HERE IN THE HOLY EUCHARIST IN THE FULLNESS OF YOUR HUMANITY, WITH ALL THAT MAKES YOU, YOU—INCLUDING THE DEEPEST SENSITIVITY OF YOUR HUMAN HEART.

DEAR JESUS, THE CHURCH TELLS US DEVOTIONS TO YOUR SACRED HEART IS DEVOTION TO YOU IN THE HOLY EUCHARIST. WE ARE TO RETURN YOUR LOVE FOR US BY SURRENDERING OURSELVES WITH OUR WHOLE HEARTS TO YOU. WE CANNOT DO THIS WITHOUT YOUR LOVING GRACE POURED INTO OUR SELFISH HEARTS FROM YOUR SELFLESS HEART IN THE HOLY EUCHARIST. JESUS, DIVINE LOVE, LOVING US IN THE BLESSED SACRAMENT, GIVE US THE GRACE TO LOVE YOU WITH ALL OUR HEARTS, SO THAT BY GIVING YOU OUR HEARTS HERE ON EARTH BY FAITH, YOU MAY GIVE US YOUR HEART TO POSSESS AND EMBRACE FOR ALL ETERNITY. AMEN.

INDEX

H

Hail Mary, 63
Heresy, contribution to
    sanctification of the Church, 17
Hinduism, 9
Holiness, 118–19
Holy Communion, Sacrament of,
    32, 39, 47, 65, 118, 147, 154–55
    effects of the, 59–64
    Eucharist as, 57–64
    Real Presence, as independent of,
        31–33
    Real Presence, necessity of,
        156–58
Holy Eucharist, 37
    institution of, by Christ, 10–16,
        77–80
    Jesus Christ's practice of poverty
        in, 132
    Mary as origin of, 173–74
    need to understand Catholic
        Church's teaching on, 147–51
    as presence statement, 65–70
    reason for Christ's institution of,
        as bodily presence on earth,
        77–80
    as sacrament, 47–49
    Sacred Heart as, 181–85
    as triple sacrament, 153–56
Holy Orders, 20–21, 46, 51
Holy See, decrees and directives of
    the, 162
Hope
    distinguish between trust and, 103
    divine, 103–4
    profession of, 103–8
        blessings of, in Real
            Presence, 107–8
Hopkins, Gerard Manley, 110–11
Human faith. *See* Faith

Humanae Vitae, 41
Humanity, 47
Humility, 123–29
    Christian, 123–24
    imitating Christ's, in the Real
        Presence, 126–29
    manifestations of, in Real
        Presence, 125–29
    Mary as model of, 175–77
    virtue, development of, 1
Hus, John, 21

I

Ignatius of Antioch, Saint, 14
Illuminating grace, 165–66
Imitation, 78–79, 80
    of Christ in Real Presence,
        117–22
    charity, 139–45
    humility, 123–29
    poverty, 131–37
Incarnate Omnipotence, 70, 85
Incarnation, 37, 81, 82–84, 117,
    164–65
    of Divine Mercy, 86
    origin of, 174
Innocent III (Pope), 20
Introduction to the Devout Life, 131
Irenaeus of Lyons, Saint, 15

J

Jairus, 68
Jesus Christ
    ascension of, 9–10, 82, 134, 150,
        155
    birth of, 9, 27, 77
    crucifixion of, 27, 53, 77, 134,
        155
    disciples, instructions to, 132
    early life of, 9